Further Steps in Honiton Lace

Further Steps in Honiton Lace

SUSANNE THOMPSON

B.T. Batsford Ltd · London

To Elsie Luxton MBE, from a grateful student

First published 1993

Typeset by Servis Filmsetting Ltd, Manchester
and printed in Great Britain by
Butler & Tanner Ltd, Frome, Somerset

Published by
B.T. Batsford Ltd
4 Fitzhardinge Street
London W1H 0AH

A catalogue record for this book is available from the British Library

ISBN 0 7134 6362 7

Contents

Foreword

This book continues from where my last, *Introduction to Honiton Lace*, broke off. It is not a book for beginners, but is intended for those who are familiar with flat Honiton lace and have had a little practice at making sewings, but who have not yet tackled any raised work. The designs show some of the more advanced Honiton techniques – mainly rolled and raised. The form of the book is the same as before, each section consisting of one pattern with diagrams and working instructions given in full detail, to help those who cannot attend a class. Each pattern is followed by a discussion of the working methods used, and their further application.

The photographs show the worked pieces, very much enlarged to present as much detail as possible, and I would like to thank the photographer, Peter Gamble of Hayle, for his skilled and painstaking work.

The patterns are progressive, in that techniques described earlier in the book are not always detailed again when they occur later. I would advise anyone who is completely new to raised Honiton to work through the first two patterns at least, before skipping to one of the later ones.

Lacemakers sometimes wonder where and when to raise parts of a pattern. There are no hard and fast rules on this subject. The raised ridges of Honiton lace have two functions; one is purely decorative, in that they give depth to an otherwise flat fabric by emphasizing the outlines and internal lines of a design. This can be seen in the larger flowers and leaves of 'Summer Scene' (p. 31), most of which could more easily have been made by flat methods. In addition, the raised ribs and rolls form a convenient way of carrying threads from one part of a pattern to another – for instance, in 'Rosette' (p. 21), where otherwise each little section or 'tap' would have to be finished and sewn out separately. In some fine old Honiton laces every single outline was raised, and one can only marvel at the workmanship and discipline that produced such *chefs d'œuvre*, but these are exceptional. What one usually sees is a mixture of flat edges, rolls and ribs, some with a mainly practical purpose and others added just for effect. Many people feel that this variety gives the lace a livelier, less rigid appearance. There is much scope in the interpretation of a design once the techniques are at the worker's fingertips, and for many this freedom of choice is one of the attractions of making Honiton lace.

Another query which occasionally arises concerns the use of a coarse thread. In the past, a coarse thread was rarely included in raised work, but nowadays one often sees it on the non-raised edges of sprigs, particularly where the space between the raised edge and the plain edge of a braid is fairly wide, and around the edges of leaves with raised veins.

Threads

The patterns in this book have all been made with No. 170/2 Egyptian gassed cotton from Belgium (Egyptisch Katoen). Unfortunately this does not have a manufacturer's name, but it is available from most of the larger suppliers of lacemaking materials, at the time of writing. If a different size or make of thread is used, the number of pairs quoted in the working instructions may have to be adjusted. Where a coarse thread was used, this was No. 50 sewing cotton.

Glossary of Working Methods

Back stitch

Process of using a hole twice. If hole has to be used more than twice, work fig. 1*a*, then repeat it on next visit to the hole, releasing the first loop and replacing the pin under the runners. Work fig. 1*b* the last time the hole is to be used.

Fig. 1a Beginning a back stitch. *Twist runners once round pin and work back without using edge pair.*

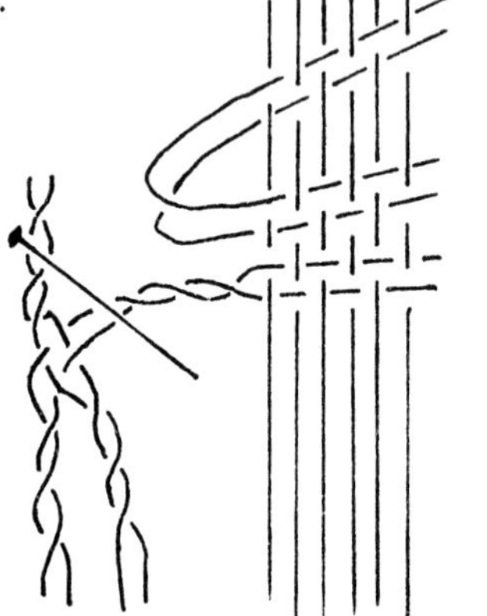

Fig. 1b Making up the back stitch. *Remove pin, releasing loop from previous row, and replace it in the same hole under the runners. Make edge stitch.*

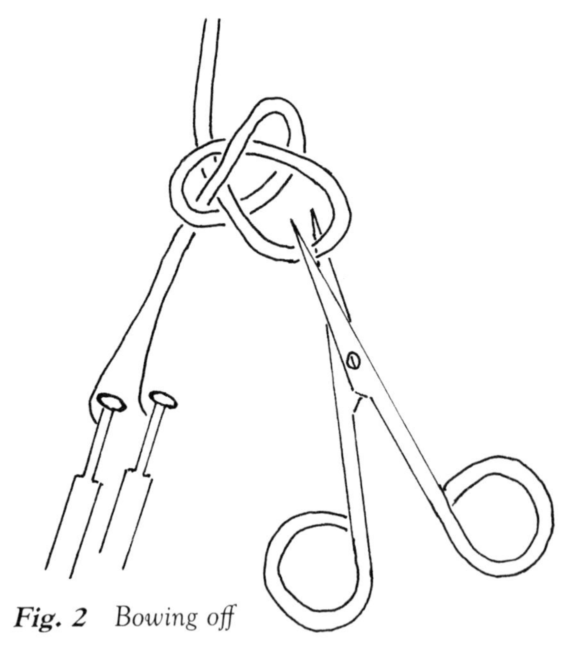

Fig. 2 *Bowing off*

Bowing off

Cutting off a pair so that the two threads are tied together at the same time. This is done by using a blunt pair of scissors (fig. 2).

Coarse pair

Made up of one coarse thread and one lace thread. The coarse pair is always worked in whole stitch.

Coarse thread

Another name for the gimp. When used, this is the outermost downright thread in Honiton braid.

Downrights

Passives

Edge stitch

Worked on the pinhole sides of Honiton braids and ribs. The runners are twisted three times and a pin is set under them, then a whole stitch and three twists are made with the runners and edge pair (fig. 3).

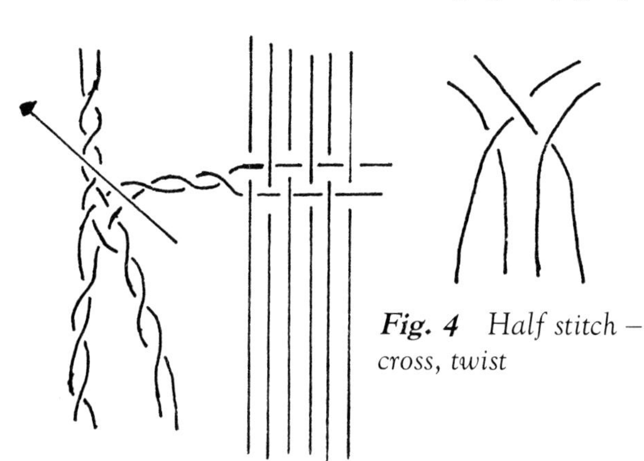

Fig. 4 *Half stitch – cross, twist*

Fig. 3 *Edge stitch*

Half stitch

Net stitch. Cross, twist (fig. 4).

Magic thread

A loop of thread laid into the work to facilitate a later sewing, at points where such a sewing is likely to be a difficult one. Double a length of lace thread and slide it under the runner pair, either before or after making the edge stitch (fig. 5*a*). Alternatively, if it is a starting pin, slide it under half the threads hanging round the pin (fig. 5*b*). Pin both the looped end and the free ends well out the way. When the sewing is to be made at this point, raise the pin, pass one of the bobbins of the pair to be sewn through the loop of the magic thread (fig. 5*c*), and pull on its free ends. The loop will come out through the pinhole, bringing a loop of the bobbin thread with it. Remove the magic thread and finish the sewing in the usual way.

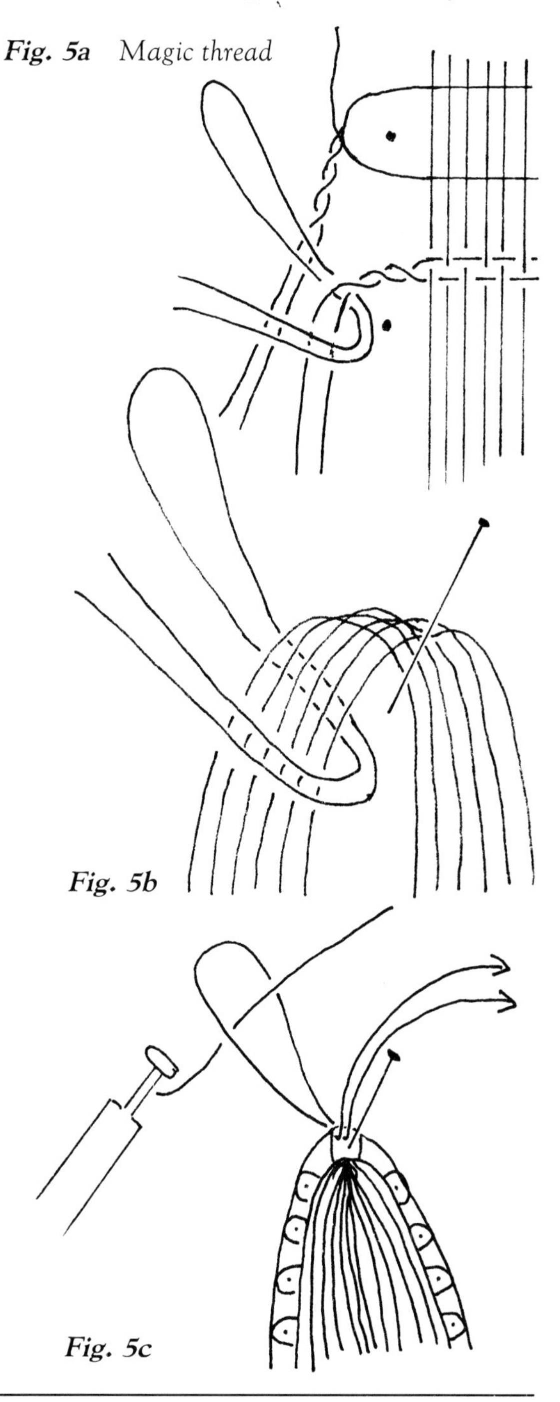

Fig. 5a *Magic thread*

Fig. 5b

Fig. 5c

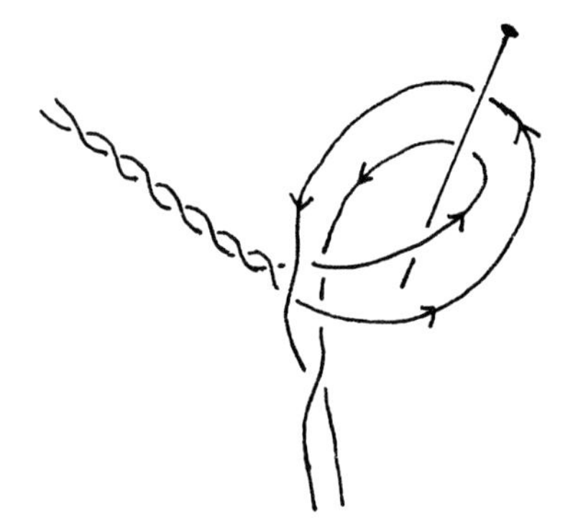

Fig. 6a *Purl in progress*

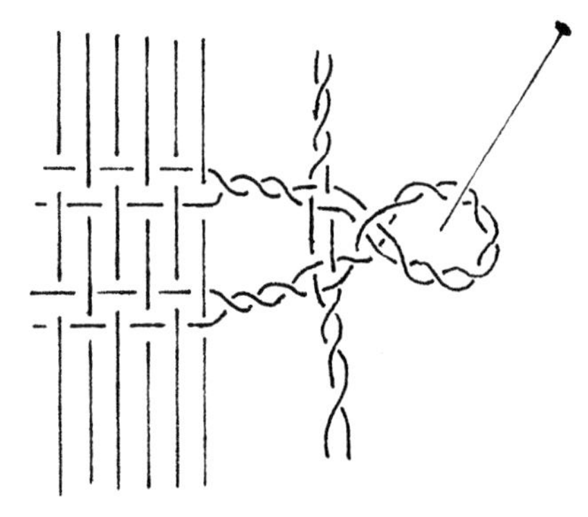

Fig. 6b *Completed purl*

Purl

Picot. After passing through the edge pair, the runners make seven twists then the purl, followed by one twist. The runners then return through the edge pair, and both pairs are twisted three times (figs 6*a* and *b*).

Rib

Ten stick or stem stitch. Narrow braid, having pinholes on one side only. On the other side turning stitches are made. (See *Turning Stitch* for alternative ways of working.)

Runners

Workers, leaders, weavers

Sewing

Attachment of a pair to a completed braid.

(*a*) *Edge sewing*: ordinary sewing or flat sewing, made round edge of braid (fig. 7*a*).

(*b*) *Top sewing*: raised sewing, made round either side bar of pinhole (fig. 7*b*).

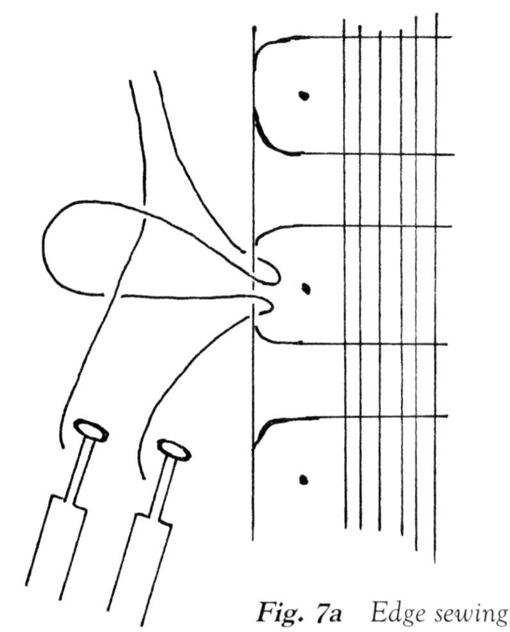

Fig. 7a *Edge sewing*

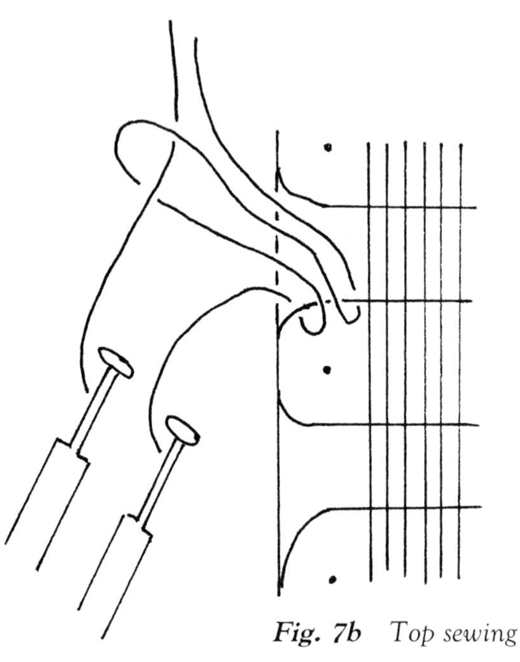

Fig. 7b *Top sewing*

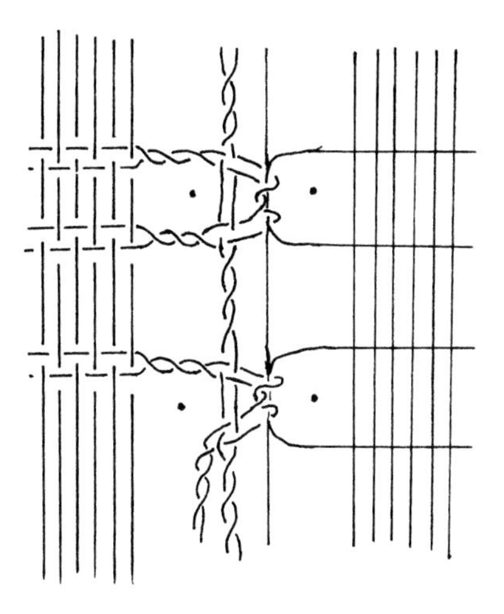

Fig. 8 Sewing to join two edges

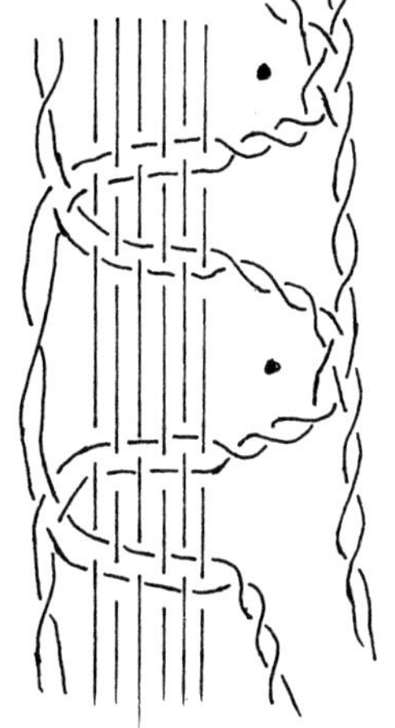

Fig. 9a Turning stitch a

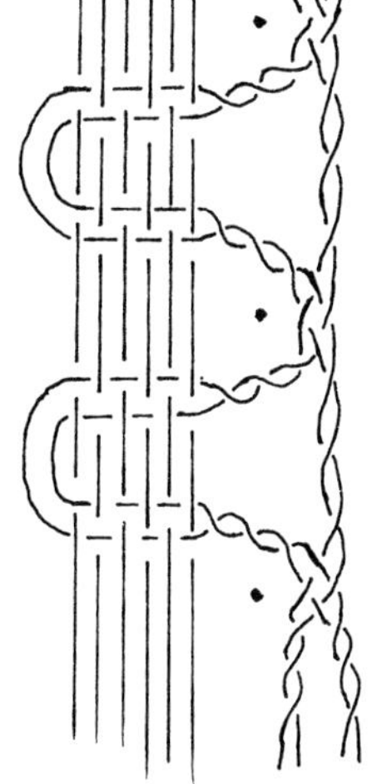

Fig. 9b Turning stitch b

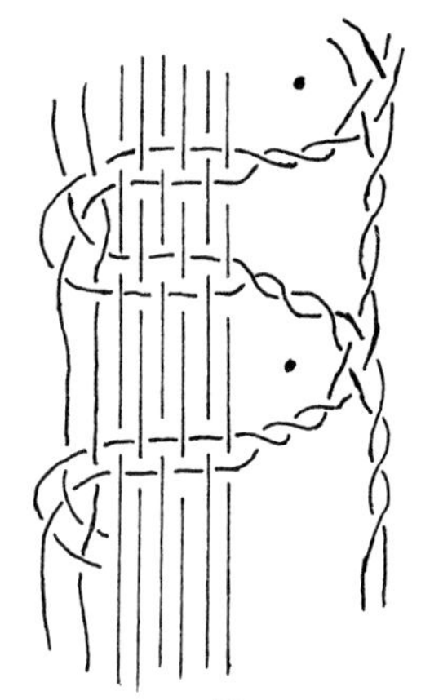

Fig. 9c Turning stitch c

Sewing to join two edges

After setting the pin, make a whole stitch with the edge pair, but do not twist either pair. Sew the outer pair to the nearest hole of the neighbouring braid with an edge sewing, then make a whole stitch with this and the next pair. Twist both pairs three times (fig. 8).

Turning stitch

Made on the plain side of a rib. There are many varieties, of which *a* and *b* below are the most popular for Honiton lace; *c* also has a following. The turning stitch used in this book is that described under *b*.

(*a*) Work to the plain side, twist the runners once and leave them. Work back with the next pair (fig. 9*a*).

(*b*) Work to the plain side, then work back with the same runners, i.e., the runners make two whole stitches with the last downright pair (fig. 9*b*).

(*c*) Work to the plain side, making a whole stitch and a reversed half stitch with the last pair (cross, twist, cross, twist, cross). The inner of these two pairs works back (fig. 9*c*).

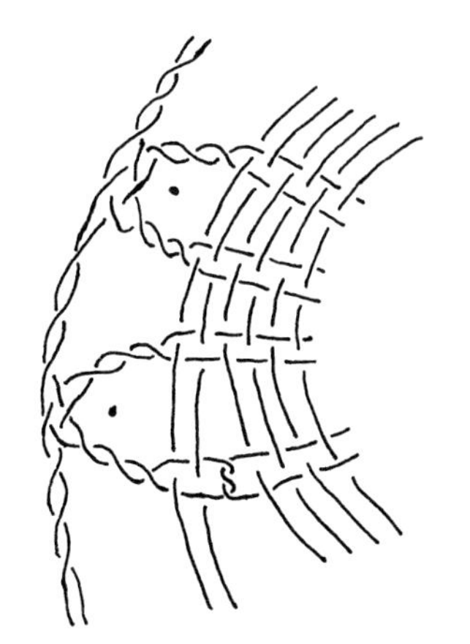

Fig. 10 Tying the runners

Fig. 11 Whole stitch

Tying the runners

A single knot made with the runners when they have passed back through the first downright (or coarse) pair, after making an edge stitch or sewing. Made at points where the clothwork might otherwise pull away from the edge (fig. 10).

Whole stitch

Cloth stitch or linen stitch. Cross, twist, cross (fig. 11).

–1–
Leaf Spray

Set up at the bottom end of the stalk with seven pairs, and rib up the stalk, making pinholes on the left. At 1 (fig. 14) change the side on which the pinholes are made (fig. 15) and continue the rib up the right side of the centre leaf. Before making the edge stitch at 2 hang in a new pair, as described below. This pair is not included in the rib but is laid back, and will be brought into use when the leaf has been turned.

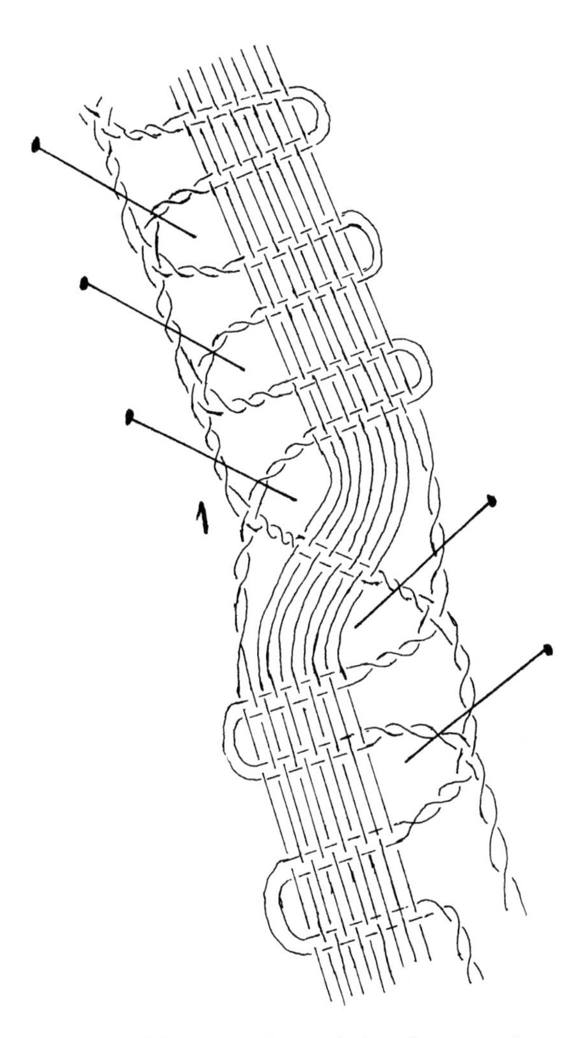

Fig. 15 *Changing the pinhole side on a rib*

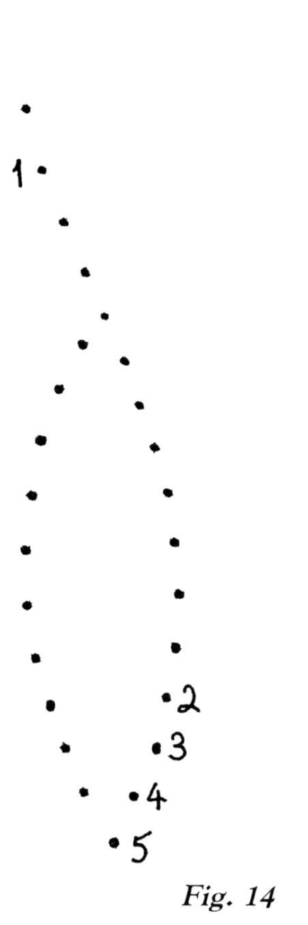

Fig. 14

Fig. 13 *Pricking for Leaf Spray*

Fig. 12 (left) *Leaf Spray*

Hanging in new pairs for later use (before the edge stitch)

Slide the thread between the bobbins of the new pair under the runners and bring the pair round the back of the pin from the outside in, in the usual way, then place the new pair to the back of the pillow. Make the edge stitch (fig. 16).

Continue the rib to 3 and hang in and lay back another new pair, laying this to the left (as you look at it) of the pair hung in at 2. Continue the rib to 4 and, after making the edge stitch, lay back a pair from the rib (see below), placing this pair to the left of the pair hung in at 3.

Laying out pairs from a rib for later use

Having made the edge stitch, and before working back, take the first downright pair next to the pin and lay it to the back of the pillow (fig. 17).

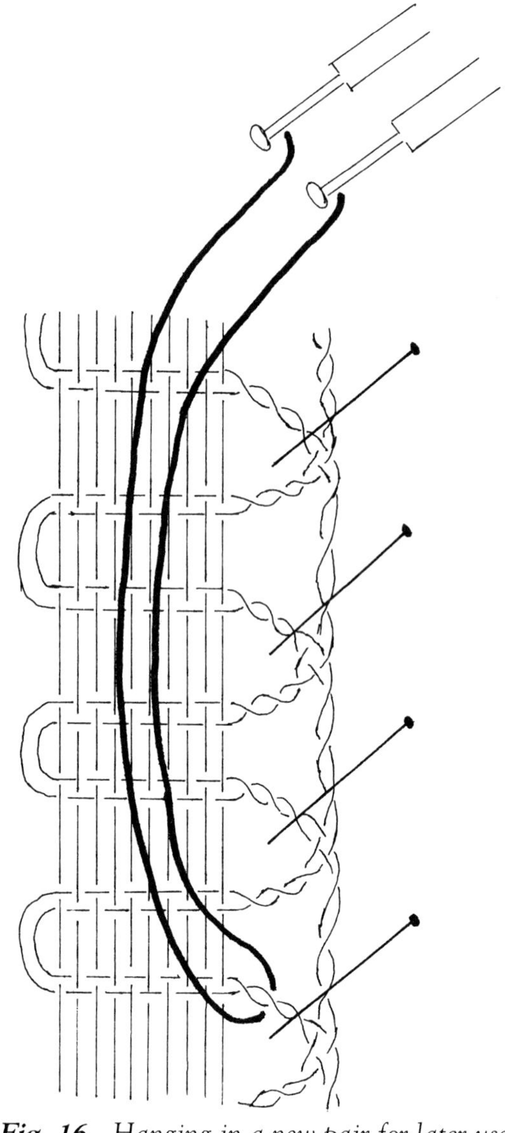

Fig. 16 *Hanging in a new pair for later use*

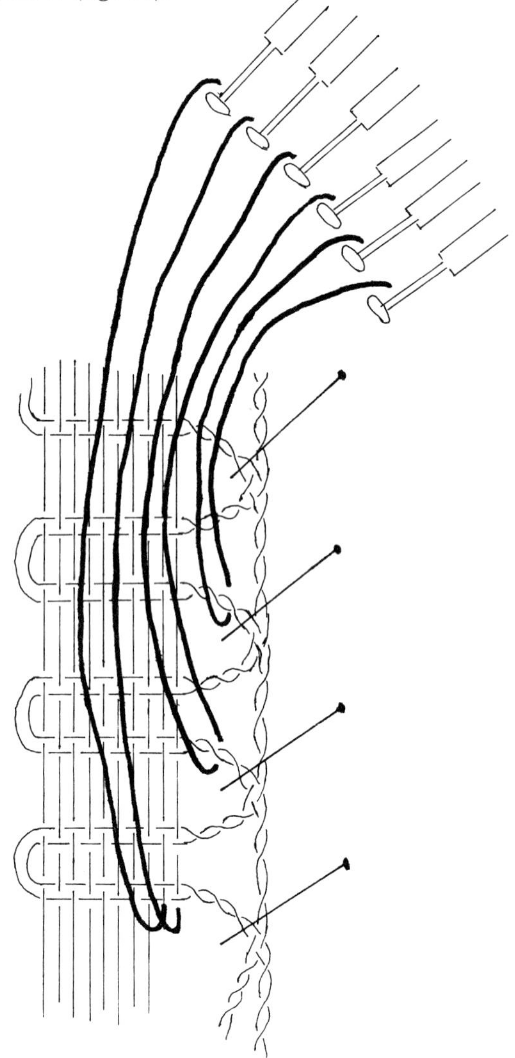

Fig. 17 *Laying out a pair from a rib for later use*

Work the rib to 5, and after making the edge stitch here, turn the pillow and tidy the pins (remove every alternate pin and push the remaining ones down into the pillow, leaving the last three or four pins standing). The pairs which were put back will now lie to the left of the six pairs in use.

Work the runners from 5 through the first downright pair and tie them, making sure that the knot sits well up against the inside of the pin. Whole-stitch the tied runners through the remaining three downright pairs, and also through the pair which was laid back at 4. Leave the runners. Tie a

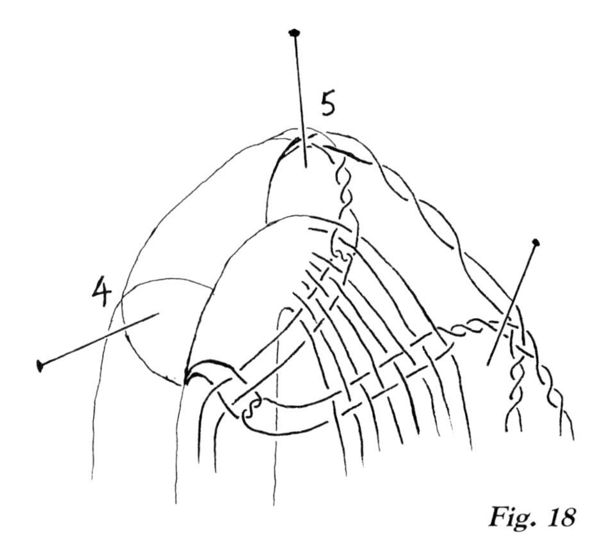

Fig. 18

single knot firmly with the pair from 4 to keep the runners in place; *these now become a downright pair, and the tied pair are used as runners to work in whole stitch to the right edge*, where they make the usual pin and edge stitch. (In fig. 18 the rib is shown only in outline for the sake of clarity.)

Work towards the rib side again, going through the downrights and the old runners, and through the pair which was laid back from 3. Tie a single knot firmly with the pair from 3 to keep the runners in place, and repeat * to *, hanging in a new pair at the next hole on the right-hand edge, and laying this pair down inside the first downright thread, as there is no coarse thread (fig. 19). In the next row the runners work through all pairs, including the pair laid back from 2. This pair is tied and becomes the new runner pair as before.

From now on the runners have to be top-sewn (*see* Glossary, *Sewing*) each time they reach the rib side, beginning at 1 (fig. 20). Do not twist the runners, either before or

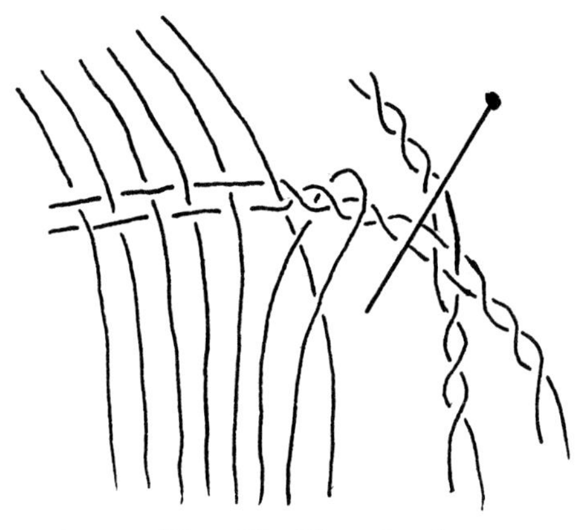

Fig. 19 *Hanging in a new pair*

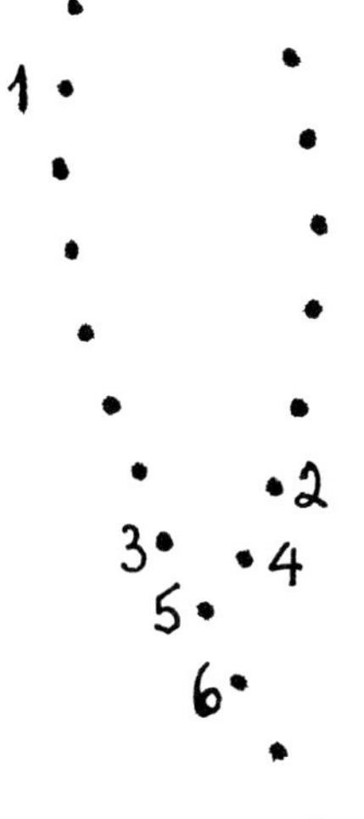

Fig. 20

after the sewing. Do not miss any of the rib holes. Remember to replace the pin after each sewing and, if you have sewn into the upper bar of the pinhole, make sure that the sewn runners are not inadvertently brought round the outside of the pin before working back (fig. 21).

runners round the upper bar of 5. Sew out the outer left downright pair round the lower bar of 5, leave the next downright pair unsewn, and sew out the next pair round the same bar. The right edge pair is sewn out into the upper bar of 6. Replace pins 5 and 6, pulling the sewn pairs (including the single unsewn pair) over to the right side of the leaf in order to leave the pinhole edge on the rib side clear. Lay aside the last two pairs that were thrown back on the left side of the leaf, and bow off the other three pairs that were thrown back, trimming the ends off close to the work. Tidy the pins. Tie and bunch the sewn-out pairs (including the unsewn pair in the bunch after tying it) in the usual way. Open

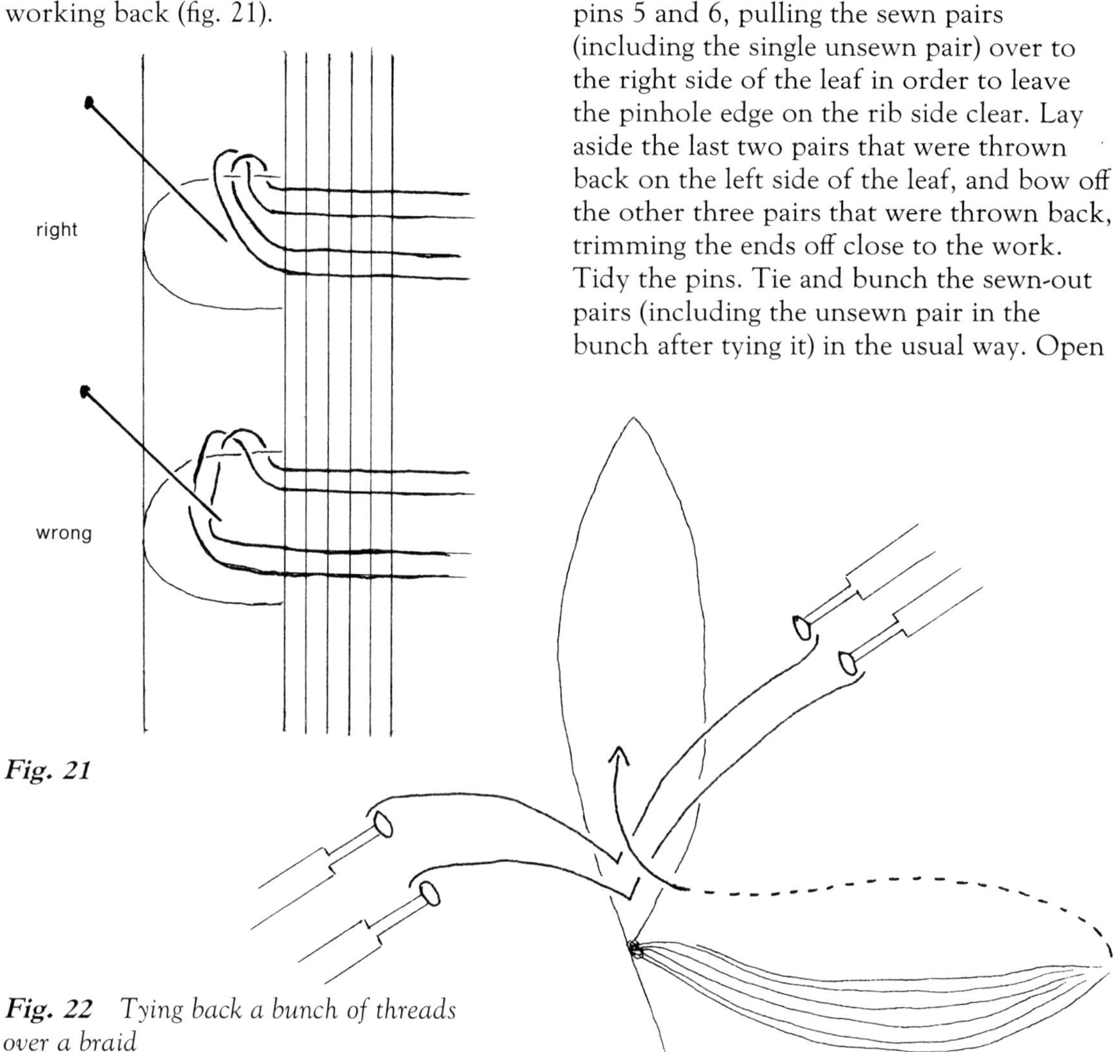

Fig. 21

Fig. 22 *Tying back a bunch of threads over a braid*

After making the edge stitch at 2, lay back the second and third downright threads from the left. After the sewing at 3 and again after the edge stitch at 4, lay back the second and third downright threads from each side. Work through the remaining three downright pairs and sew out the the two pairs that were laid aside, placing one bobbin from each pair on each side of the leaf (fig. 22). Lay the bunch back over the leaf and tie each of the opened-out pairs three times over the bunch. Bow off the bobbins, and trim the ends close to the knots.

Work the whole stitch leaf of the pair below the completed leaf. Top-sew the pairs needed for the rib into hole 1 (fig. 23), three pairs round one bar, four pairs round the other; each set may be attached with only one sewing here (figs. 24*a*, *b* and *c*). Lay the pairs over the plain side of the stalk and rib the lower edge of the leaf. Follow the instructions for the first leaf – the same number of pairs are used, the only

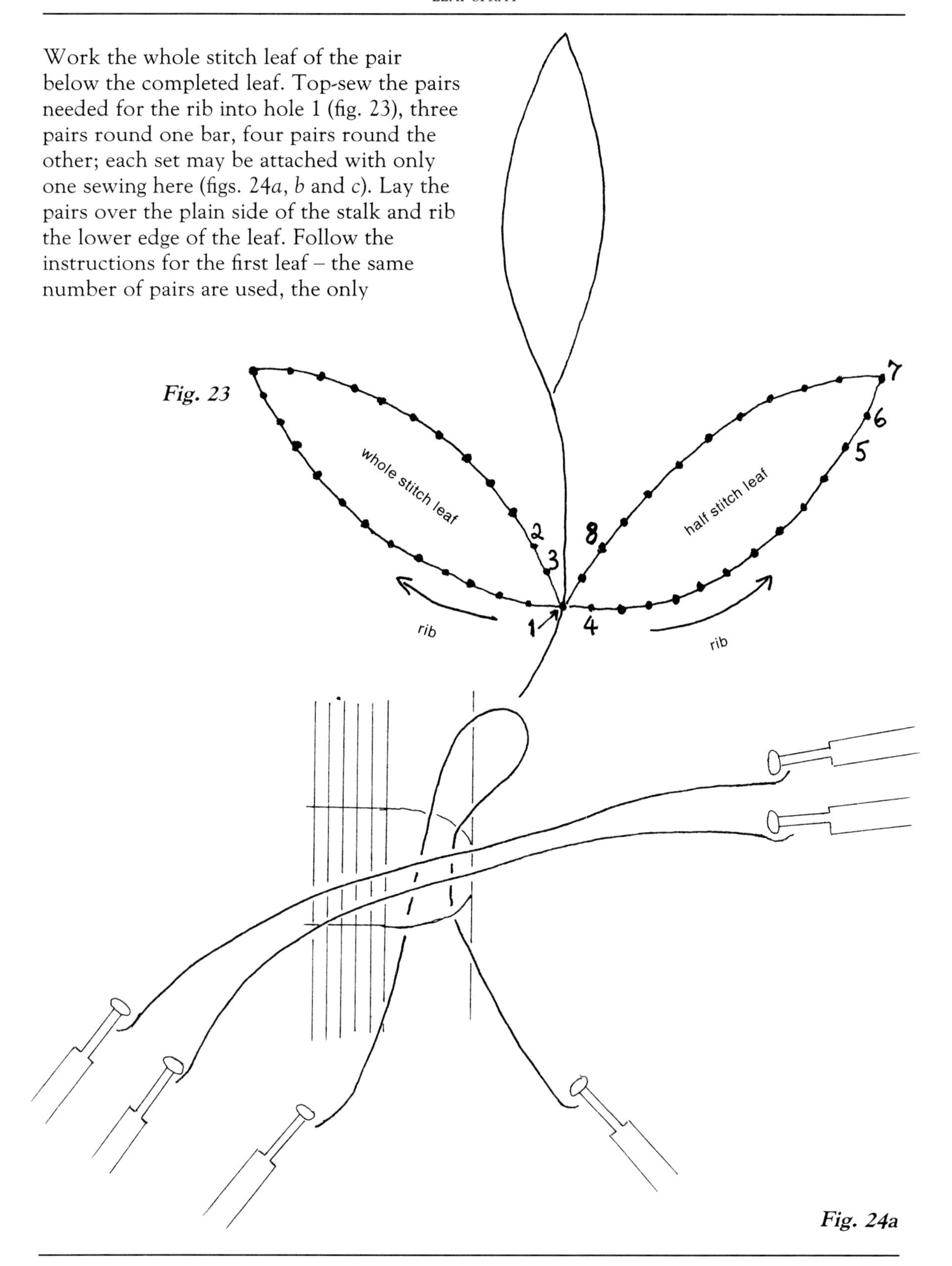

Fig. 23

Fig. 24a

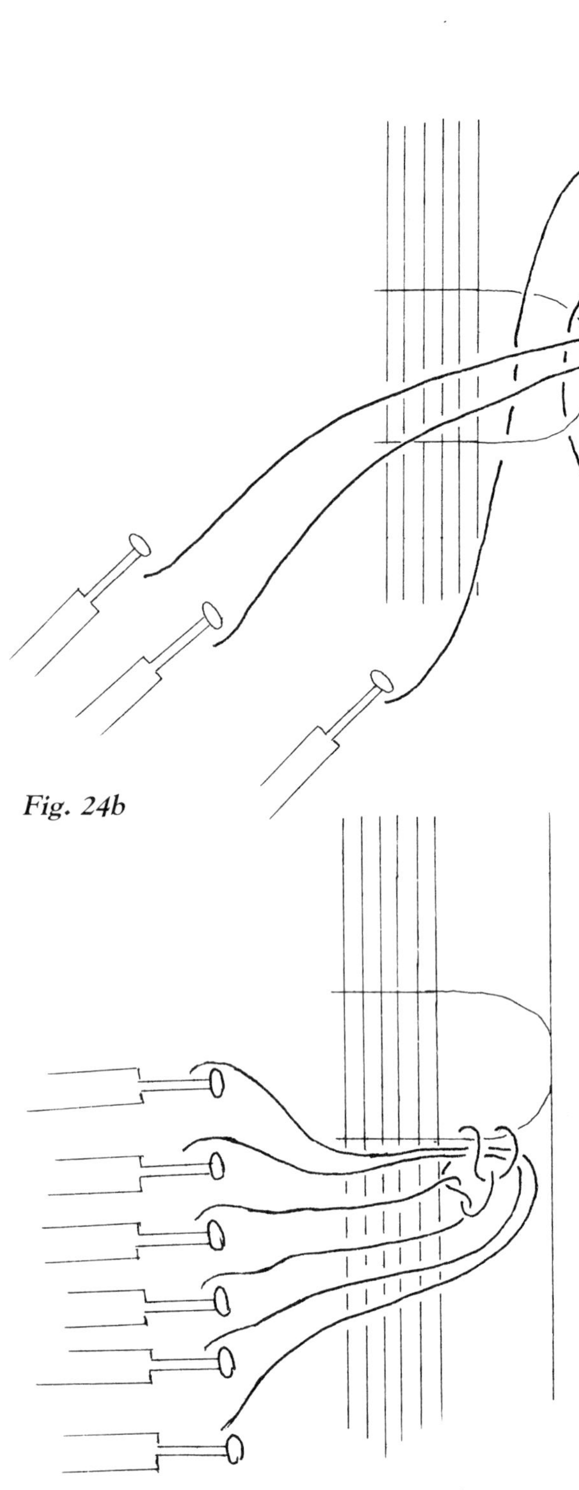

Fig. 24b

Fig. 24c *Attaching several pairs with one top sewing*

difference is that a vein is made down the middle by twisting the runners.

Make a back stitch (*see* Glossary) at 2 and throw back a pair in each of the next three rows to reduce the number to seven again. Do not miss hole 3 – it is probably hidden under the stem rib. From 3 work through the downrights to 1 and make an edge sewing (*see* Glossary, *Sewing*) here. Tie the sewn pair once, twist it three times and leave it. Take the edge pair from 3 as runners, work them through the downrights to 4, set the pin and make the edge stitch with the sewn, twisted pair. Work rib along the lower edge of the opposite leaf, keeping pinholes on the left. As this leaf is to be worked in half stitch, it will not be necessary to add any more pairs. Instead, lay back a pair from the rib at 5 and one at 6, placing this pair to the right of the pair laid back from the previous hole.

Turn the pillow after the edge stitch at 7 and tidy the pins. The two pairs that were laid back will now lie on the right of the bobbins in use. Work in whole stitch through the first downright pair and tie the runners. Work the tied runners in half stitch through the next two downright pairs, and in whole stitch through the pair laid back from 6. Leave the runners. Tie the pair from 6 firmly and use it as new runners to work in half stitch towards the left edge through two downright pairs, and in whole stitch through the last downright pair. Work the next edge hole.

Return in whole stitch through the first downright pair, in half stitch through the next three pairs, and in whole stitch through the pair from 5. Leave the runners. Tie the pair from 5 firmly and use it as new runners to work towards the left edge through three downright pairs in half stitch, and in whole stitch through the last downright pair. Work the next edge hole.

From now on top sewings will have to be made each time the runners reach the rib side, beginning at the hole next to 5. Make a whole stitch with the outermost downright pair on both sides in every row, and half stitches with the pairs in between. Make a back stitch at 8, and in the last few rows gradually remove three pairs. (Remember to make a whole stitch with both the outer downright pair, and the pair inside it, where the pair is to be discarded. Then take the second and third downright bobbins, i.e. the two middle bobbins of the two whole stitch pairs, tie these three times and lay them back.) After the last sewing at 4, work the runners in whole stitch once more to the pinhole side and sew these, the edge pair, and one of the downright pairs into the hole immediately above 1 on the main stem (edge sewings). It will be necessary to remove quite a number of pins from the base of the whole stitch leaf and from the main stem, and to bend back the standing pins, in order to gain access to this hole, but the sewings are not particularly difficult. Tie, bunch and cut off.

The next pair of leaves is begun like the last, but as these are a little wider, more pairs will be needed. The whole stitch leaf uses twelve pairs; begin hanging in one hole earlier on the rib side, so that three new pairs are hung in and one pair is laid back out of the rib. On the pinhole side one new pair is hung in at each of two consecutive holes after the top of the leaf has been turned. Make a back stitch on the pinhole side near the bottom of the leaf, and gradually reduce to seven pairs before crossing over and ribbing up the lower side of the half stitch leaf.

This leaf is made with nine pairs. Begin adding pairs three holes from the top of the leaf, hanging in and laying back one pair at each of the first two holes, and laying back a pair from the rib at the last hole before the top. Turn and work back as before, making top sewings when all the laid-back pairs have been used. Make a back stitch near the end and reduce the number to four or five pairs before sewing out.

Working Methods

Pointed shape raised on one side

To decide where to begin hanging in and laying back pairs for later use, imagine how far you would be hanging in new pairs if you had started at the point and were working the shape by the normal flat Honiton method. The last pin at which a new pair would be hung in using the flat method (fig. 25) would be the first pin from which a pair is laid back on a raised edge.

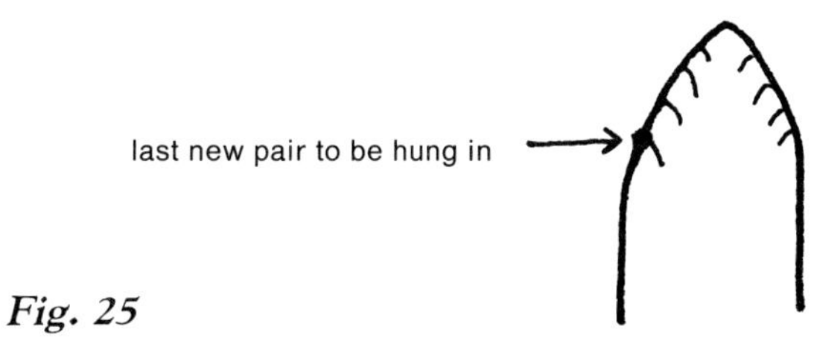

Fig. 25

Laying out pairs from a rib for later use

Whether and where to do this depends on the thickness of the rib and on the shape being worked. If the shape comes to a very narrow point (fig. 26*a*), too many pairs left in the rib when the tip is reached would look clumsy. However, in a shape like fig. 26*b*, no pairs would be laid back at all from the rib; instead a new pair would be hung in and laid back at every hole except that at the tip.

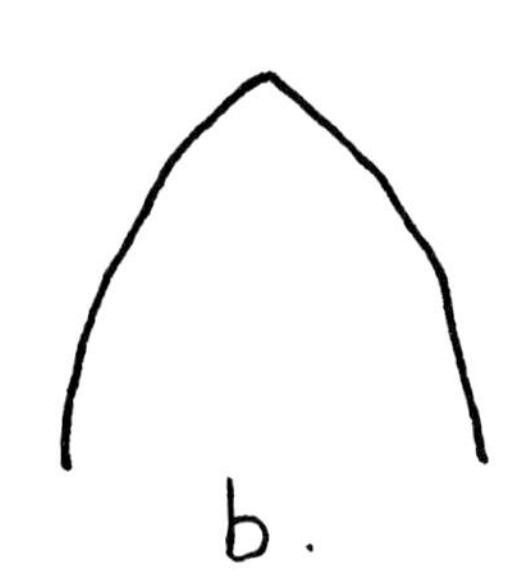

Fig. 26

Uneven clothwork

Beginners sometimes find small holes appearing at the places where pairs that were laid back are tied and brought into use as runners. This could be either because the knot was not tied firmly enough, or (and more likely) because the runners that were abandoned here have been pulled and have dragged the knot down. After tying the knot, give another little tug to the old runners in the direction in which they have been travelling, and then gently tighten the knot again. Try to avoid pulling the abandoned runners for several rows after they have become passive – not very easy if your tension is good.

Some workers like to place the abandoned runners out over the pin from which the new pair is hanging, so that they do not drag on it while it is being tied and the first row is worked. This is quite satisfactory provided one remembers to replace the old runner pair before the next row!

If small holes persist in spite of all your efforts, the problem can be avoided by sewing the runners into the rib when they have passed through the new pair. In that case the new pair is not tied, but enters the clothwork as a downright pair and, after being sewn, the runners work back to the pinhole side.

Honiton half stitch braid

A development in recent years has been the omission of the twist given to the runners at the beginning of the row, after they have passed through the whole stitch (or coarse) pair. This seems to have very little effect on the appearance of the braid. Some workers feel that it gives a closer connection between the straight pair and the fabric. Both methods are in use at present.

Fig. 27 (right) *Rosette*

— 2 —

Rosette

The method of working leaves, butterflies' and birds' wings, etc. in little sections called 'taps' is typical of raised and rolled Honiton lace. The motif, composed of five leaves, is designed to fit into a 7.5 cm (3 in.) diameter frame, box lid or paperweight, but for the purpose of learning the technique a single leaf can be made, and this would fit into a brooch, pendant frame or key-ring. To make a single leaf, hang seven pairs round a pin in hole 1 and work in rib up the middle vein of the leaf, keeping pinholes on the right and laying in two magic threads at the hole following 1. Then continue from * in the following instructions.

To work the whole motif

Hang seven pairs round pin 1 (fig. 29), at the same time laying in two magic threads (*see* Glossary), and rib clockwise round the central ring, keeping pinholes on the outer side. After the last pin, work one more row,

Fig. 29

Fig. 28 *Pricking for Rosette*

taking the runners to the plain side. Sew the runners and also the edge pair on the pinhole side into 1, using the magic threads. Tie both sewn pairs twice. Lay all the threads to the right of the rib just made, ready to work the mid-rib of the tap leaf. If you have raised pin 1 before joining the circle, be careful that the threads do not accidentally become hooked round this pin; they should all come out on the pinhole side between the last pin of the ring and pin 1. These pairs are used to rib up the centre vein of the leaf, with pinholes on the right. Give three twists to the first pair on the right, to be used as an edge pair, and use the outermost pair on the left as runners to work towards the right. Lay in two magic threads at the first pin. Continue the rib.

*Hang in and lay back a pair at 2 (fig. 16, p. 14). At 3, two new pairs are hung in and laid back – one before the edge stitch, and the other after the edge stitch has been made. This second pair is simply looped round the runners (second pair from edge) and laid back beside the first pair without first being guided round the pin (fig. 30). Hang in and lay back a new pair at 4 and, when the edge stitch has been made, lay back a pair from the rib (fig. 17, p. 14). Rib to 5 and make the edge stitch. Tidy the pins, leaving the last four or five standing, and turn the pillow. The pairs which were laid back now lie on the left of the rib pairs.

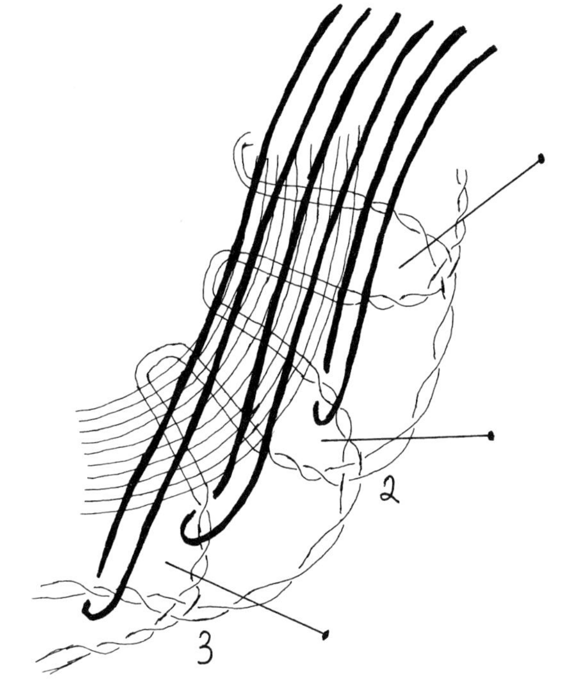

Fig. 30

Work through the first downright pair and tie the runners. Work the tied runners through the remaining rib pairs, and also through all the pairs that were laid back. Leave the runners, tie the last pair they passed through, and use the tied pair as new

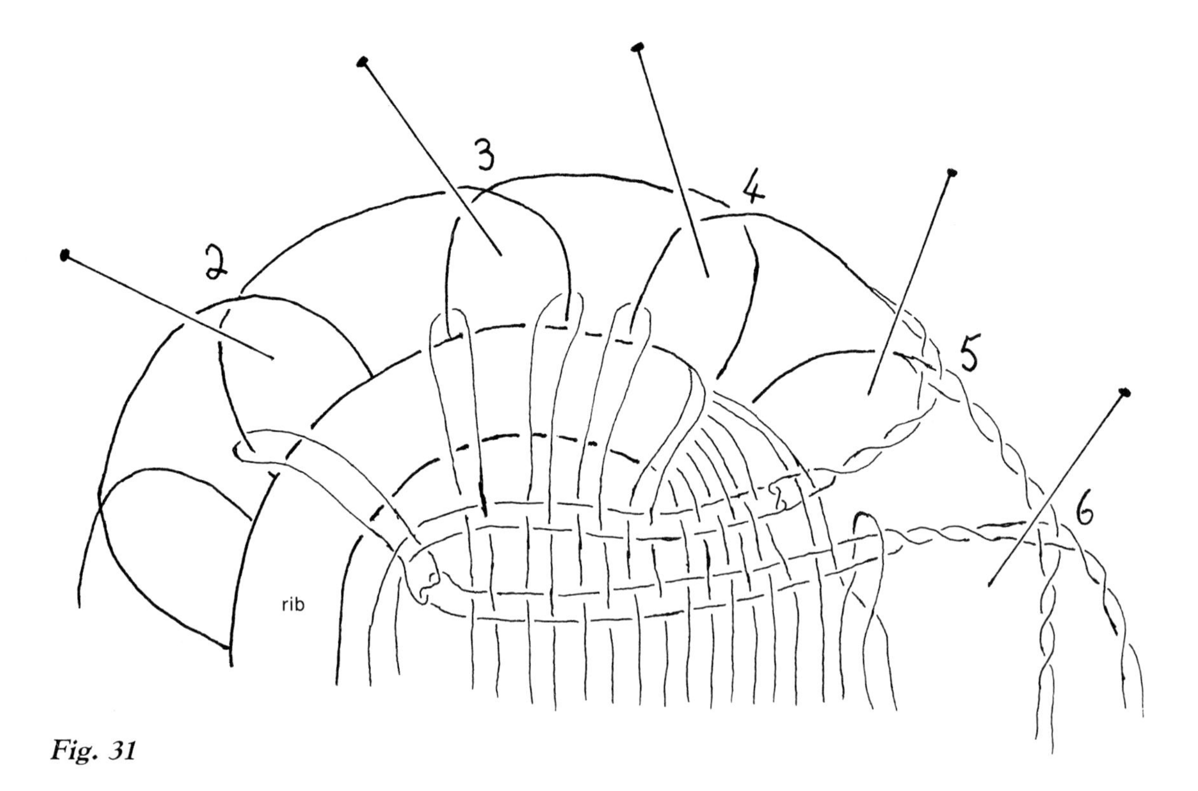

Fig. 31

runners to work to 6. Hang in a new pair here (fig. 31 – twelve pairs altogether). Tie the runners again at the beginning of the next row.

Continue working down the tap, making top sewings on the rib side – the first of these into the hole below 2. One or two back stitches will be needed on the pinhole side near the end, so that when the bottom of the tap is reached it will be possible to work from the last pinhole 7 (do not miss this hole: it is almost hidden by the rib) to 8, a little below the level of 7. At the same time gradually reduce the bobbins to seven pairs, throwing out the last of these surplus pairs in, or just above, the last row. Do not cut off this pair but lay it aside for possible use later.

**Tie the sewn runners at 8 twice, then pick up the remaining six pairs, lay them between the bobbins of the tied pair, and tie this pair again twice over the bunch. Do not cut off. Tidy the pins, bow off all the discarded pairs (except the last pair that was set aside) and trim the ends off short.

The pairs are now 'rolled' up along the edge of the tap. Take one pair out of the bunch and lay it aside. Take another pair in one hand (usually the pair that was tied over the bunch, unless this has a knot coming up). Take the remainder of the bunch in the other hand and wind the single pair repeatedly and closely round the bunch, making a tight roll to reach to 9. To make the roll neat and even, it helps to have all the bobbins in the bunch level. Sew the winding pair with an edge sewing at 9, tie it twice, twist it and leave it on the right of the roll pairs; it will be the edge pair for the next section of rib (fig. 32). Replace pin 9.

The pair left out at the beginning of the roll is now used to sew the roll to the holes along the side of the tap; when doing so, miss hole 7. Remove the pin from 10.

*Insert the needlepin into the hole and bring it out under the edge of the braid and under the roll (fig. 33*a*). Hook through one of the threads of the sewing pair (fig. 33*b*)

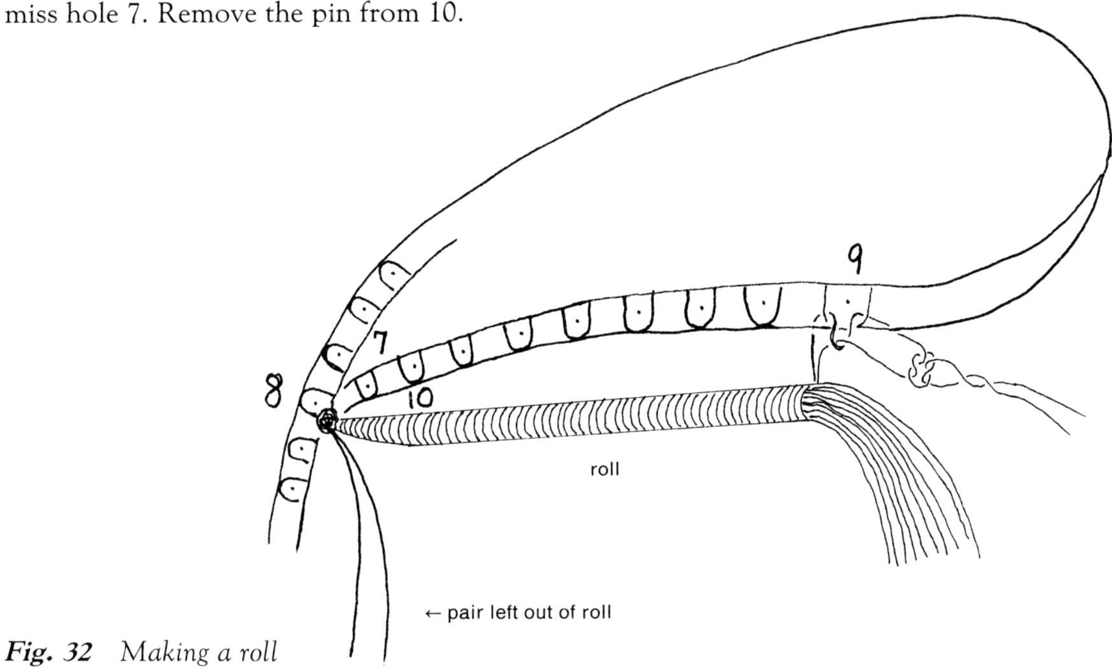

Fig. 32 *Making a roll*

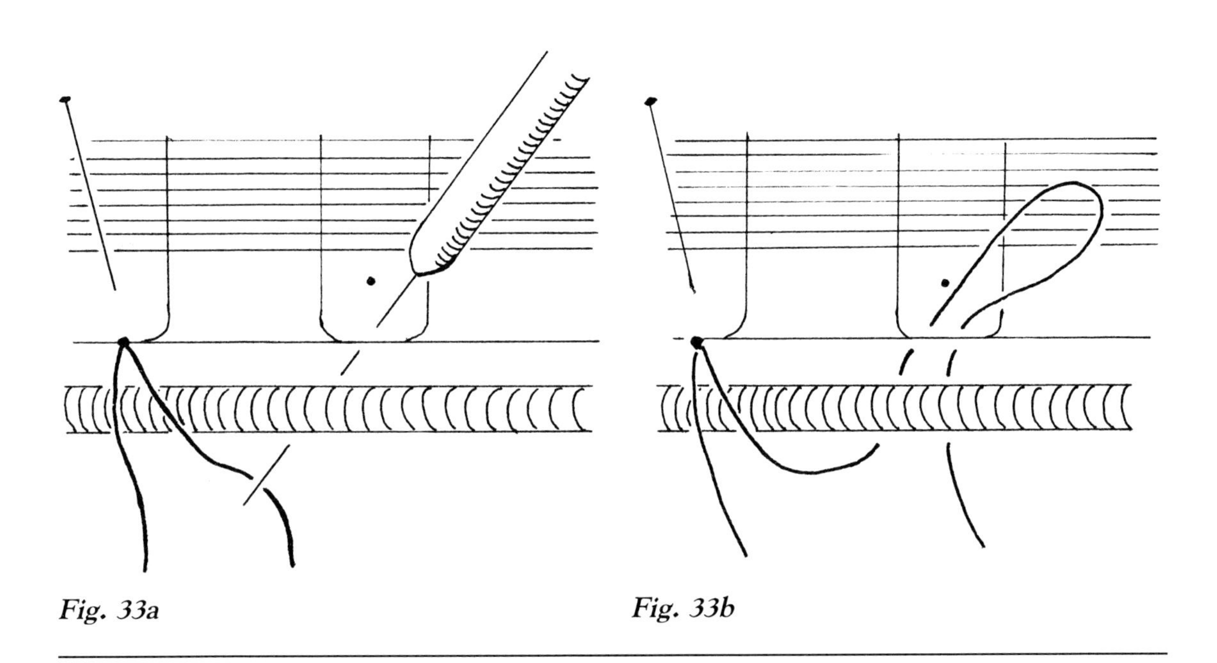

Fig. 33a

Fig. 33b

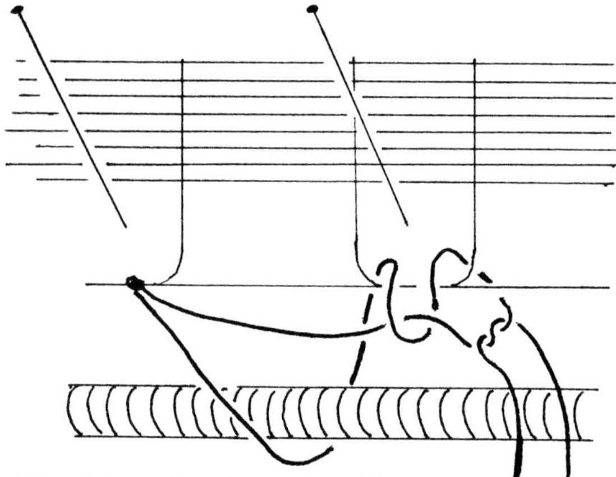

Fig. 33c *Attaching the roll*

and pass the other bobbin through the loop. Pull up and tie the pair once. Replace the pin (fig. 33c). Remove the pin from the next hole and repeat from *, sewing into every hole along the side of the tap and making the last sewing into the hole before 9. Tie the sewn pair twice here and lay it to the left of the roll pairs.

The pairs are now used to make a rib along the top of the next tap. Sort out the threads from the roll (they become twisted during the making of the roll) so that they lie reasonably flat. Work the pair used to sew the roll as runners through the roll pairs to the right, twist it** and set pin 11 under it. Hang in and lay back a new pair, and make the edge stitch with the twisted pair that was left at 9. Continue the rib, hanging in and laying back two pairs at 12. At 13 hang in and lay back a new pair, and also lay back a pair from the rib. Rib to 14, turn the pillow and tidy the pins.

Work through the first downright pair, tie the runners and work through all remaining pairs. Leave the runners to become passive, tie the last pair they passed through (the pair hung in at 11) and use this pair as runners to work to 15. Hang in a new pair here, and again tie the runners at the beginning of the next row (twelve pairs). Continue the tap, making pinholes on the right and top

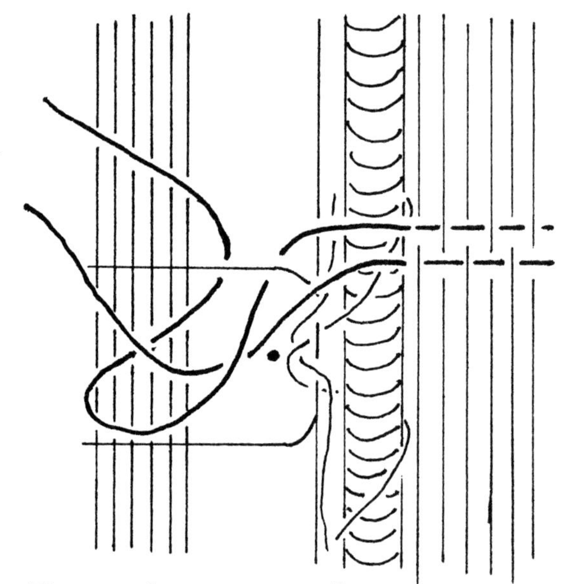

Fig. 34 *Sewing over a roll*

sewings on the left, the first of these at the hole below 9. Simply ignore the roll on this side – do not sew round it (fig. 34); it will show as a little raised ridge on the right side when the piece comes off the pillow.

Four back stitches are needed near the end of the tap to keep the weaving level. After sewing into 7, work to the pinhole side and, before returning, bring down the pair laid out and set aside at the end of the last tap, to fill in the little gap which often occurs at this point. Lay this pair between the bobbins of the outermost downright pair on the left, work the next row and sew the runners at 8 on the mid-rib. The sewings are now made into the mid-rib. Gradually reduce the number of pairs to seven again, throwing out pairs from the right side (i.e. the inner side of the curve) for preference, if there are no knots coming up. Discard the last of these pairs in or just before the last row and set it aside. The last row is worked from 16 to the sewing at 17. Replace the pins after sewings, for the sake of tension and to preserve the holes of the mid-rib. These will all be used again when the half stitch section is made.

Work the next roll similarly, repeating ** to ** above, 16 and 17 corresponding with 7 and 8, and 18 corresponding with 9. This tap is a little more sloping at the top, and slightly narrower than the last. Hang in and lay back a new pair at 19 and 20; after the edge stitch at 20, lay back a pair from the rib. Rib to 21, turn the pillow and tidy the pins. Work as for the last tap, hanging in a new pair at 22 (ten pairs). The last row is worked from 23 to 24; this time set aside the last two pairs to be discarded, as the gap in the next tap is likely to be a large one.

When making the roll for the lowest tap, sew in the winding pair at 25. Hang in and lay back two pairs each at 26 and 27, rib to 28, turn the pillow and tidy the pins (eleven pairs). Work through the first downright pair, tie the runners, then work through all remaining pairs and sew the runners into the hole below 25. It will be necessary to back-stitch at every hole, beginning at 29. The two discarded pairs set aside in the last tap are brought in one at a time before the sewings at 23 and 24. Gradually reduce the number of pairs to seven again. After making up the back stitch at 30, work to 31, sew, and tie the sewn pair twice. Sew the edge pair on the other side to 32 by means of one of the magic threads, and tie it twice. The threads should all lie over the mid-rib between pins 31 and 32. Bunch the downright bobbins, cross the two tied pairs under the bunch and tie them twice over the bunch. Do not cut off. Tidy the pins, cut off all discarded pairs and trim the ends short.

The seven bunched pairs now make a roll up the side of the mid-rib, working as before. Remember to leave one pair out of the bunch before beginning the winding. It will be found easier to estimate the length of the roll if the pins along the mid-rib are raised; the roll can then be laid against the pins every now and then while it is being made. Sew in the winding pair at 1 (fig. 35), tie it twice, twist it and leave it lying on the left of the bunch pairs. Attach the roll as before, sewing into every hole of the mid-rib, making the last sewing at 2 and tying the pair twice after this sewing. Use this pair as runners to work through the bunch threads (after these have been straightened) to 3, where a new pair is hung in and laid back. Make the edge stitch with the twisted pair from 1 and continue the rib, laying back a pair from the rib at 4, 5 and 6 (eight pairs). Rib to 7 and turn the pillow.

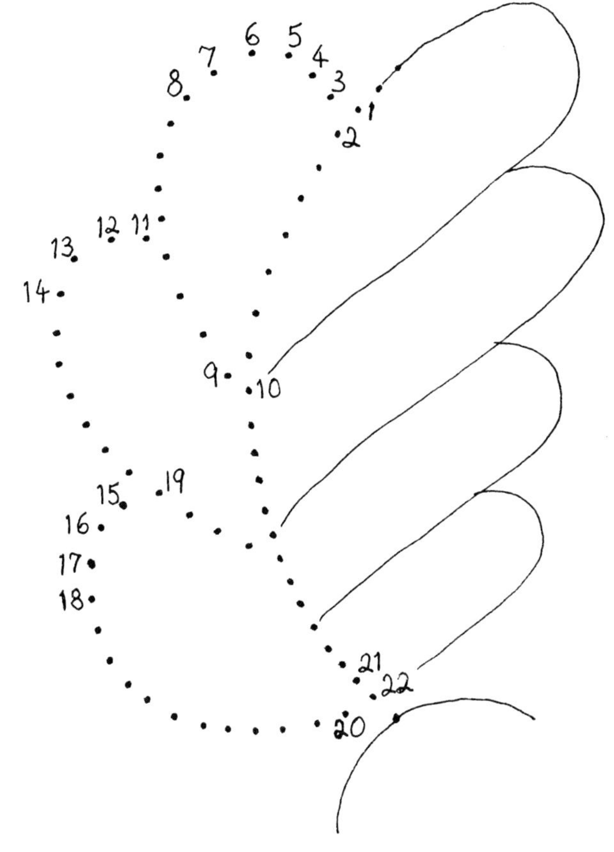

Fig. 35

Make a whole stitch with the first downright pair, tie the runners and continue across the row in half stitch through all except the last pair (hung in at 3). Work through this pair in whole stitch and leave the runners. Tie the pair from 3 firmly and use it as runners to work in half stitch through all except the last downright pair, which is worked in whole stitch. Make the edge at 8 and continue the tap, making top sewings on the right – the first one at 2 – and pinholes on the left, working in half stitch with a whole stitch through the first and last downright pair in each row. There is no need to reserve a pair to fill in the gap in the next tap, as half stitch stretches obligingly to fill in odd little corners. Remove one pair before the end of the tap. It may also be necessary to make a back stitch, so that the row after 9 slants down to 10 – this last row is worked in whole stitch. Sew the runners at 10, tie, bunch and roll up the side of the tap.

The next tap is made with nine pairs. Hang in and lay back a new pair at 11. At 12 hang in a new pair and also lay back a pair from the rib. Lay back another pair from the rib at 13. Rib to 14 and turn the pillow. Continue the tap, repeating * to * above, but also tying the runners at 10 (*see* Glossary, *Tying the Runners*) and throwing out two pairs, to reduce to seven pairs again before the end of the tap.

For the last tap hang in and lay back one new pair at 15, and one new pair and one pair out of the rib at each of 16 and 17. Rib to 18 and turn the pillow (ten pairs). Work through all pairs (making a whole stitch with the first and last) and sew the runners at 19. Continue the tap as before, but reduce the number of pairs gradually until only four or five pairs remain at the end. Arrange the rows so that after pin 20, holes 21 and 22 are still available. Work the last row in whole stitch and sew the runners, and perhaps one middle downright pair, at 21. Sew the edge pair to 22, using the remaining magic thread. Tie all sewn and unsewn pairs three times. Ensure that all these pairs are lying between pins 21 and 22 over the whole stitch part of the leaf. Bunch the downrights, cross the two outer sewn pairs under the bunch, tie them three times over the bunch and cut off.

Sew seven pairs into the equivalent of hole 1 (fig. 29) at the base of the next tap leaf, making three or four sewings and laying in the extra pairs needed, as shown in fig. 24. Work as for the last leaf. Where the taps come close to the previous leaf, join at one or two holes (*see* Glossary, *Sewing to Join Two Edges*).

Filling

This is 'Pin and Stitch'. Position the pillow so that there is a horizontal row of three holes across the top. The numerals in fig. 36 show the number of pairs and the places where they are to be sewn in (top sewings). Two pairs cross with a whole stitch and three twists; a pin is set between them and covered with a whole stitch and three twists. The pairs then divide and travel diagonally to a hole in the row below, where they meet pairs from a neighbouring pin. If preferred, the centre pin can be replaced with a leadwork, as in the model, fig. 27. X marks the holes where the pairs are sewn out.

Working Methods

Hanging in pairs for later use along a horizontal line

The tops of the taps in this pattern are slightly flattened, and in such places it is usually necessary to hang in and lay back at least two pairs at each hole, unless they are being worked in half stitch. Whether these are all new pairs, or whether some of them are laid back from the rib, depends on the number of pairs in the rib and on the shape

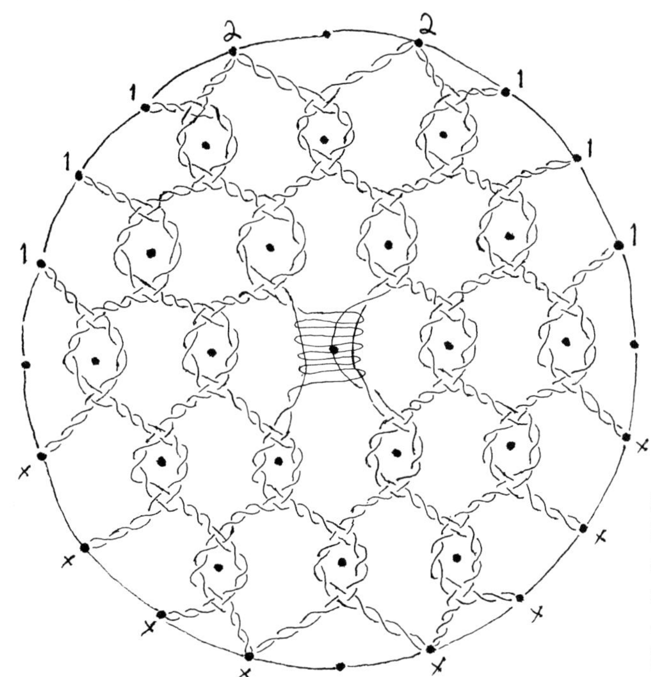

Fig. 36 Pin and Stitch filling

of the tap. The aim should be to hang in sufficient pairs to produce the desired density of clothwork and, if necessary, to reduce the thickness of the rib a little so that, when the pillow is turned, not too many pairs are left hanging on the pinhole side of the tap.

When the pillow has been turned, it is advisable to check that the hung-in pairs are still lying in order. Some workers like to tie the new pairs with a single knot before bringing them into use (to stop them from sliding), and some like to give a preliminary twist to the new pairs when working in half stitch, but neither of these methods is really necessary.

Working the tops of taps

How far the rib is worked across the top of the tap before turning, and how far the first row is to be worked once the pillow has been turned, depends on the shape of the top and on the relative position of the

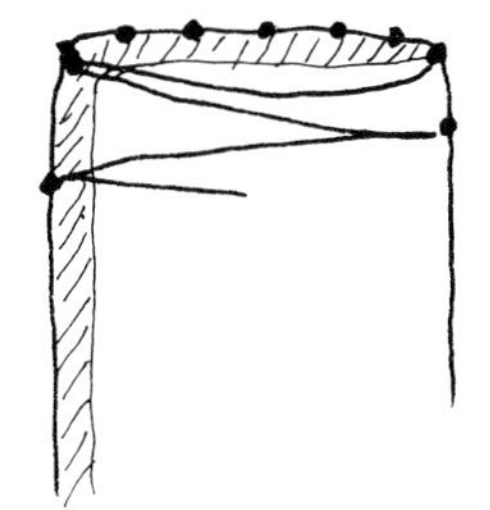

Fig. 37a

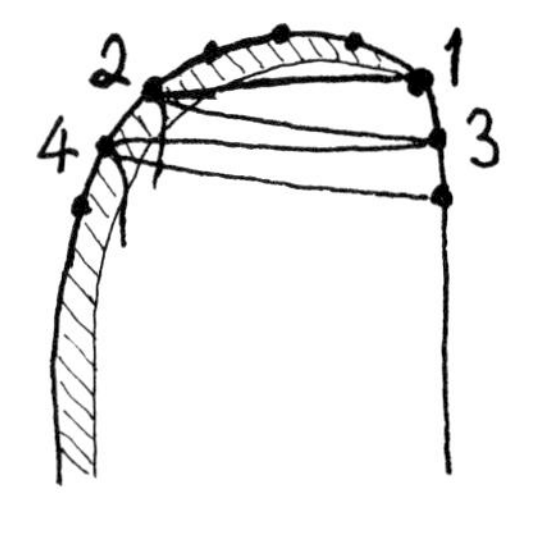

Fig. 37b

pinholes. If the shape is rectangular, as in fig. 37*a*, the rib would be worked straight across the top to the outermost pinhole on the far side and, after turning, the runners would go through all the hung-in pairs and be sewn on the rib side.

If the shape is slightly rounded, as in fig. 37*b*, work the rib to a point from which a level row can be woven across the tap to a hole that is either level with, or slightly above, the next hole on the pinhole side. In fig. 37*b* this must be hole 1, and the first row goes as far as 2. If the rib had been continued to 3 and the first row had been worked to 2, the weaving would have slanted too much; if the first row had been worked from 3 to 4, there would have been a gap between the rib and this row. If, on the other hand, the weaving had been worked from 1 to 4, there would again have been a gap and the weaving would have slanted too much the other way. Having said this, note that occasionally the weaving of a tap is deliberately begun on a slant in order to avoid making a back stitch further down.

Working the ends of taps

At the bottom of the tap, always arrange the rows of weaving so that the last sewing is slightly below the last pin worked on the pinhole side. Some workers like to insert a magic thread at the last hole on the pinhole side (looping it round the runners after the edge stitch has been made), and this undoubtedly facilitates sewing at this rather awkward point when the next tap is being made. However, the looped thread tends to get in the way unless it is firmly pinned down over the finished part of the work, and covered.

Rolls

When the rolls have been made in this pattern, the winding pair is normally sewn in one hole above the hole from which the taps diverge, so producing a more natural-looking curve at the junction of the taps. However, this is not an invariable practice. Sometimes the winding pair is sewn into the hole at the junction of the taps, thus giving a deeper indentation between the taps. This is also done where the new tap pulls away sharply from the previously worked one, as in fig. 38. Whichever place is chosen for

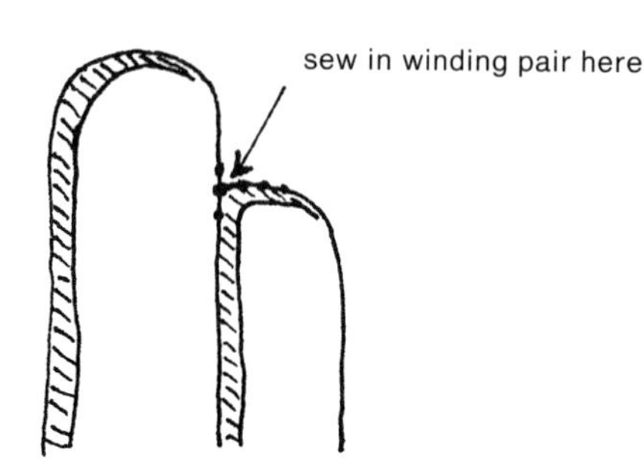

Fig. 38

this sewing, lay the bobbins of the roll close along the edge of the previous tap, so that their weight will not drag on the winding pair while it is being sewn and tied. This makes for an easier sewing and a closer join.

There are two schools of thought on where to finish sewing in the pair that attaches the roll to the edge. Some workers like to make the last sewing in the same hole in which the winding pair finished, and others like to make it in the hole before. Which is best depends to some extent on the position of the first hole of the subsequent rib, and on the number of pairs in the roll, but both methods seem to give a satisfactory result and workers can make their own choice.

Magic thread

This is often used, as in this pattern, at a starting hole, i.e. where a number of threads are hung round a pin. If working with an odd number of pairs, insert the magic thread *before* the pairs are twisted, preparatory to beginning the work.

Although magic threads do make awkward sewings much easier, the lacemaker would be well advised not to rely on them too much but to get some experience with difficult sewings, because sooner or later one forgets to put in a magic thread. Some sewings, particularly those which must be done without removing the pin, soon become no harder than ordinary sewings, given a little practice.

Tap leaf with a single ridge along the middle

In this pattern the tap leaf had a double ridge for the mid-rib, made by the rib and the subsequent roll. If only a single ridge is desired, the pairs must be sewn out and cut off at the end of the first side of the leaf, and sewn in again at the top of the other side. Another way of making a tap leaf all in one piece but with a single mid-rib is described on pages 102–4.

Fig. 39 (right) *Summer Scene*

—3—

Summer Scene

Fig. 40 Pricking for Summer Scene

Large flower

Begin by hanging seven pairs (and two magic threads) round a pin set in the arrowed hole (fig. 41). Rib clockwise round the central ring. Join as in the last pattern and continue the rib, pinholes on the right, up the side of the petal. Work clockwise along the top until the edge stitch at 1 has been made, and leave. The little raised vein which marks the indentation at the centre of the petal is made next.

*Leave aside the three outer pairs (the runners, edge pair and first downright pair). Twist the next pair three times. Use the last downright pair on the left as runners to work through two pairs to the right, twist it three times, set pin 2 under it (fig. 42), and make the edge stitch with the twisted pair. Continue the rib with these four pairs, working the next two holes, 3 and 4. After the edge stitch at 4, work once more to the plain side and tie the runners twice. Spread the tied runners apart, lift the other three pairs, lay them down between the runner bobbins and tie the runners again twice over the bunch.

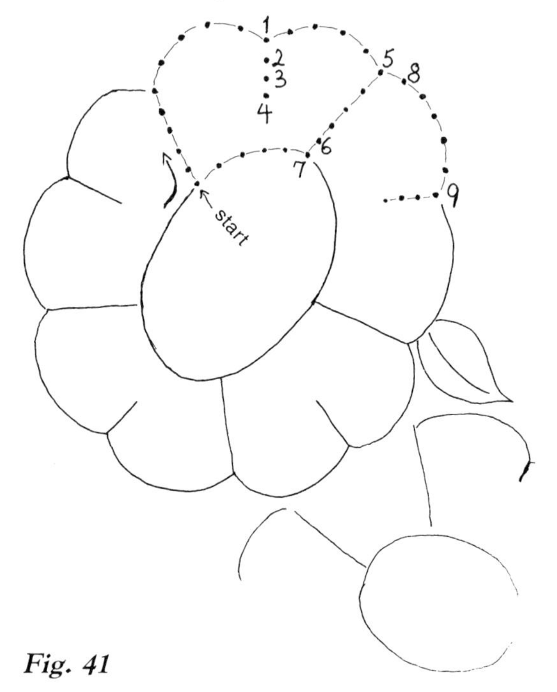

Fig. 41

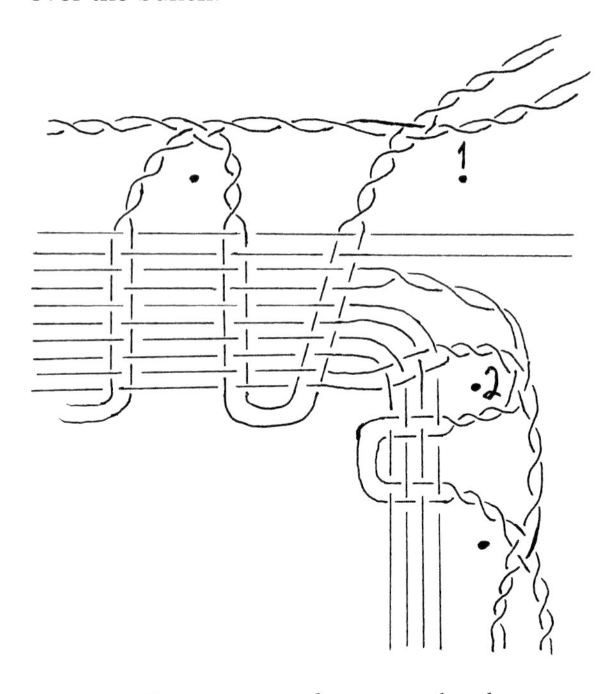

Fig. 42 Beginning a side vein on the plain side of a rib

These four pairs are now rolled back up the side of the small rib. This can be done as in the last pattern, i.e. leaving one pair behind to attach the roll. However, an alternative method was used here: take the tied pair in one hand, and the other three pairs in the other hand, and wind the tied pair two or three times round the bunch. Sew the winding pair at 3 (edge sewing), tie it twice,

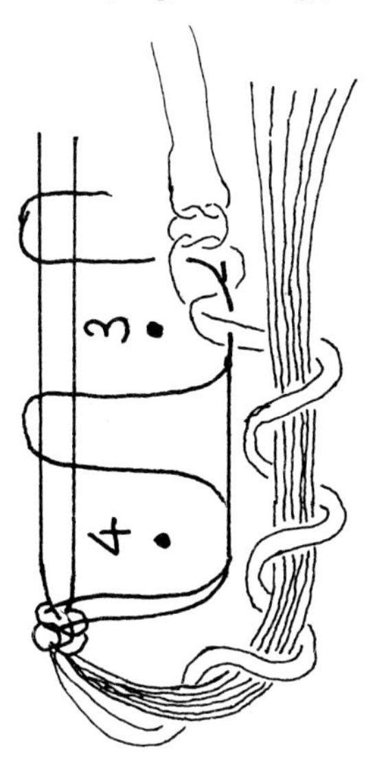

Fig. 43

wind it again two or three times round the bunch, sew it at 2, and tie it twice (fig. 43). Remember to replace pins 2 and 3. Now pick up all four pairs and lay them in between the bobbins of the downright pair, which was laid aside at 1. Tie this pair twice over the bunch and continue the rib along the outer edge of the petal, using the runners left waiting at 1.

After the edge stitch at 5 (fig. 41), tie the runners and continue the rib with all seven pairs down the side of the petal towards the centre circle, making a rather thicker division between the petals. After the edge stitch at 6, work through to the plain side, top-sew the runners to the left bar of hole 7, tie them twice and leave them on one side. Top-sew the edge pair on the other side to the right bar of 7 and tie it twice.

Lay the remaining five pairs between the bobbins of the tied edge pair, tie it twice again over the bunch, then use it as a winding pair to make a roll with the bunched pairs, as in the last pattern. Sew the winding pair with an edge sewing at 5, tie it twice, twist it three times and leave it to become an edge pair. Use the other sewn pair from 7 to attach the roll, tying it once after each sewing and twice after the last sewing, also at 5. Use this pair as runners to work through all but the twisted pair on the other side, and make hole 8. Continue the rib along the outer edge of the next petal until the edge stitch at 9 has been made. This corresponds with 1. Repeat from * all round the flower.

After the last pinhole, work the runners through to the plain side, make the turning stitch, work back through all but the edge pair and sew the runners with an edge sewing at 1 (fig. 44). Sew the edge pair into the same hole. Tie both these pairs twice and leave aside. The rest of the rib pairs are now rolled down the side of the first petal, making a diminishing roll as one pair is left behind at each hole. They can then be used for the half stitch filling.

Fig. 44

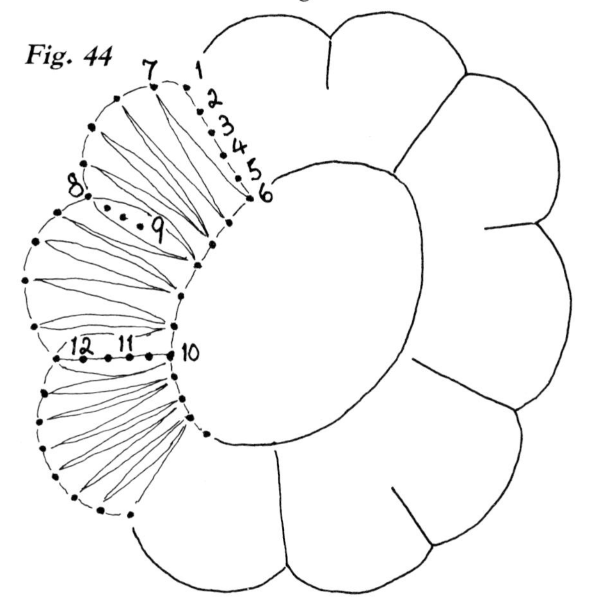

Diminishing roll

*Take one pair of the remaining rib pairs, wind it twice round the other pairs and sew it with an edge sewing at 2. Tie it twice and leave it aside. Repeat from * for holes 3, 4 and 5. Sew the last pair at 6 without removing the pin, and tie it twice. Top-sew a new pair at 2, 3 and 4 to give ten pairs altogether. The filling is then worked anti-clockwise round the flower. Using the pair from 6 as runners, make a whole stitch with the nearest pair, tie the runners once and continue in half stitch, making a whole stitch with the last pair. Sew the runners at 7. Continue working in half stitch, following the course shown in fig. 44 and making top sewings on both sides, until the sewing at 8 has been made. Leave the runners here and make a join to the little raised vein.

Lift pin 9 and re-position it in the hole. If it has been leaning slightly to the right, make it lean to the left, or vice versa. This enlarges the hole a little and makes it easier to do the sewing without removing the pin. Sew the fifth pair from the right to this hole. Do not tie this pair but check and, if necessary, correct the position of the threads – hold the pair, one bobbin in each hand, spread them a little apart and pull them gently. The slight tension on these threads will show whether they are lying in the right order, i.e. the thread that was running towards the left side before the join should now lie on the left side of its partner. It will then run in the same direction when work is resumed.

Remove any other pins from the vein, and remove pin 9 when two or three more rows have been worked. Continue the half stitch filling until the sewing at 10 has been made. Here the work has to be joined again to the rib between the two petals and, as this is a slightly longer rib, it is best to join at two places. Instructions are given this time as an example, but usually lacemakers use their judgement, choosing which holes to join to and picking pairs that lie naturally over these places to do the sewings. Top-sew the third downright pair from the right (not counting the runners) to the right bar of 11, and the third pair from the left to the right bar of 12. Again, do not tie these pairs but check, as above, that the threads are lying in the correct position. Do not leave any pins in this vein.

Continue filling in the flower, joining to the veins as you pass them. It will be necessary to sew twice into most of the holes of the centre circle in order to keep level. There is a slight tendency for sewings to pull away from the centre circle, and this can be counteracted by tying the runners every now and then. After the last sewing, work one more row in whole stitch and sew out all the pairs with top sewings into holes 1 to 6. Lay aside the innermost pair after it has been sewn and tied (it can be used in the filling). Make the remaining pairs into two bunches and cut off.

Filling

This is 'Devonshire Cutwork'. Using top sewings, sew in one new pair into each of the next five holes on the left of the pair hanging from 6. Sew one new pair in the next hole to the right of 6, and two new pairs in the next hole to the right of this hole (fig. 45). Twist all pairs three times.

Leave the first pair on the right – it will not be needed until the next row. Select the knot-free bobbin of the next pair to be the weaver and use this pair and the next pair on the left to make a very small, square leadwork, finishing with the weaver as the outside left thread. *Twist both pairs three times. Leave the right pair and, with the left pair and the next pair on the left, make a whole stitch, twisting both pairs three times. Pull up firmly, taking care that the last leadwork is not distorted. (Whilst pulling up, it helps if the side of the right wrist is rested gently on the pair of bobbins hanging from the leadwork.) Leave the right pair and with the left pair and the next pair on the left make another leadwork *using the same weaver* as for the last, which is now the third of the four threads, counting from the left. Once again finish with the weaver on the outside left. Repeat from * across the row and, after the last leadwork, finish by top-sewing the left pair, which contains the weaver, into the next free hole of the rib circle. Use the passive bobbin to make the loop of the sewing, and pass the weaver bobbin, which has been resting loosely on the pillow or with its tail tucked under one of the cover cloths, through the loop. Pull up carefully and tie the pair twice, making sure that the first of these knots does not distort the leadwork. Twist this pair three times, and leave it hanging – it will be used in the next row.

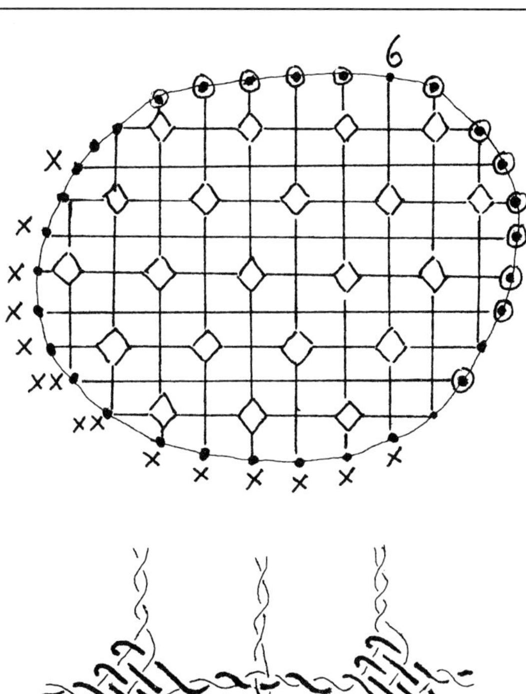

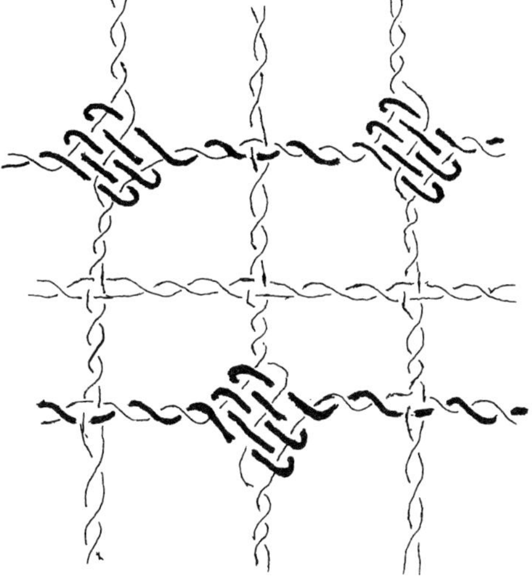

Fig. 45 Devonshire Cutwork filling

Sew in a new pair in the next free pinhole on the right, twist it two or three times, then work it in whole stitch through all pairs, twisting both pairs three times after each stitch. At the end of the row, pull up carefully, holding the travelling pair in a straight line below the previous row whilst pulling down the vertical pairs gently but firmly with the other hand. Sew out the travelling pair.

These two rows form the pattern. Complete the filling, following fig. 45; the encircled holes show where new pairs are sewn in, and holes marked X show where pairs are sewn out and are not used again. Note that the fourth and fifth leadwork rows are begun with vertical pairs which are sewn into the edge (no need to tie these after the sewing) before being brought into use again.

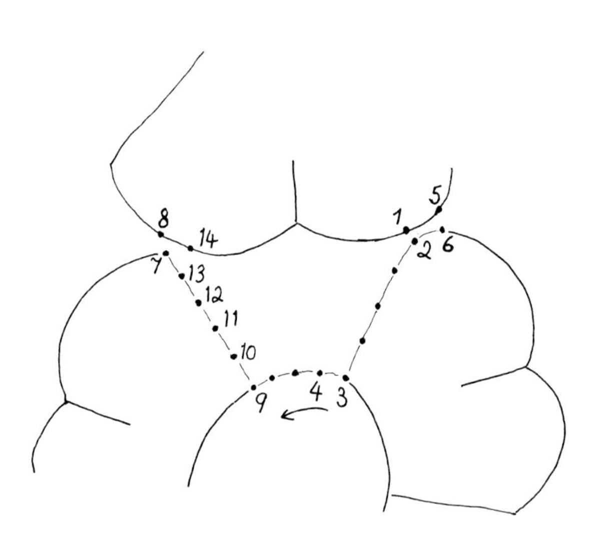

Fig. 46

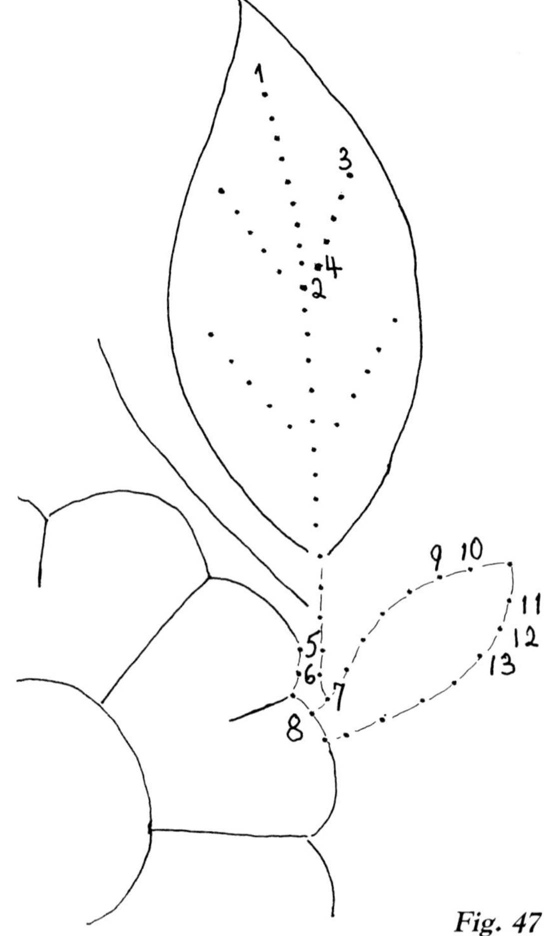

Fig. 47

Smaller flower

This has to be started differently so that the divisions between petals will match those of the large flower. Top-sew seven pairs into hole 1 (fig. 46) of the completed flower – three into one bar and four into the other. Twist the outer pair on the right three times. Use the outer pair on the left as runners, working them to the right through all but the twisted pair, and make pin 2. Rib towards the centre circle, with pinholes on the right. After making the edge stitch at 3, change the side on which the pinholes are made. To do this, give three twists to the outer pair on the left, tie the runners when they have passed through the first downright pair (necessary here because of the sharp turn), then continue the row, making hole 4 with the new edge pair.

Continue the rib, pinholes on the left, working anti-clockwise round the centre circle. After the last hole work the runners through to the plain side, sew them with an edge sewing to 3 and tie them twice. Place all bobbins except the edge pair between the bobbins of the sewn pair, which is tied twice again over the bunch. Push all the bobbins to the right side of the pillow so as to make hole 3 accessible for the sewing of the edge pair. Tie this pair twice and leave it.

Now make a roll up the side of the petal with the bunched bobbins, using the pair that was tied over the bunch as the winding pair. Sew this pair into the edge of the completed flower at 5, tying it and twisting it twice. Use the other pair from 3 to attach the roll, making the last sewing at 2. This pair now works through the bunch pairs to make pin 6 with the twisted pair from 5.

Continue the rib outline as for the last flower.

At 7 make a join to 8 (*see* Glossary, *Sewing to Join Two Edges*). Continue the rib towards the centre circle, joining to 9 as before – the runners to the left bar of 9 (tie this pair twice and lay it aside), and the edge pair to the right bar of 9. Tie the edge pair twice, twist it once or twice round the remaining pairs, sew it with an edge sewing to 10, tie it twice again and lay it aside. Make a diminishing roll as before, leaving one pair hanging from 11, 12, 13 and 7, and sewing the last pair at 8. Top-sew one new pair at 13, giving a total of eight pairs.

Work the half stitch filling with these pairs, going clockwise round the flower, beginning with the pair from 9 as runners and working the first row to a top sewing at 14. As the veins between petals are shorter in this flower, only one join will be sufficient when passing over them. Choose one of the middle pairs and join it to one of the middle holes. Complete the flower and work the filling as before.

Leaf with opposite raised veins

The raised veins are made first. Set up with seven pairs and a magic thread at 1 (fig. 47), and rib down the vein, pinholes on the right. When the edge stitch at 2 has been worked, the side veins are made, beginning with the right vein. Lift the first four downright pairs past the pin, to the right, over the edge pair and runners. Turn the pillow so that the holes of the side vein are facing you, and rib up the side vein with these four pairs, as shown in fig. 48, pinholes on the left. After the edge stitch following pin 3, work to the plain side, tie the runners twice, lift the other three pairs, lay them between the bobbins of the tied pair, and tie this twice again over the bunch. Roll these pairs back to the main

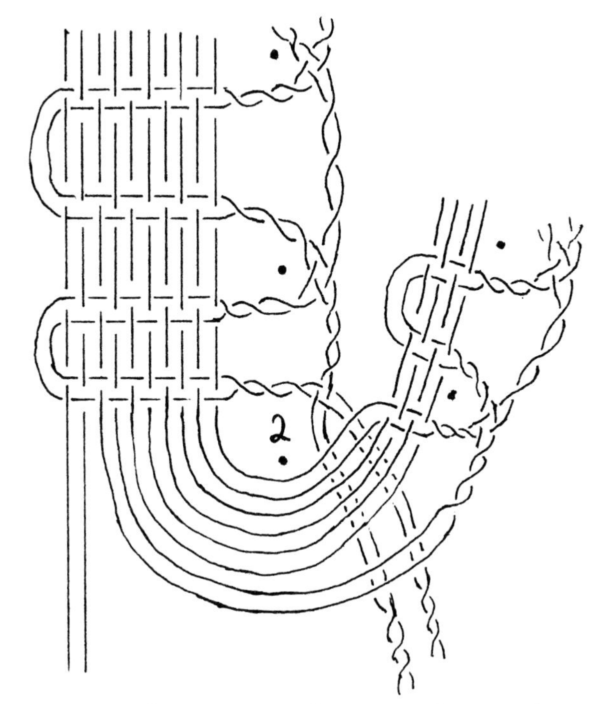

Fig. 48 *Beginning a side vein on the pinhole side of a rib (opposite side veins)*

rib, using either the method shown in fig. 43 or that shown in figs. 32 and 33. After sewing and tying at 4, lift the four pairs that have made the side vein back over the runners and edge pair, and lay them down between the bobbins of the downright pair not used for making the side vein. Tie this pair twice over the bunch; it does not matter whether the tied pair is then laid down to the left or to the right of the bunch, or even if one bobbin is laid on each side.

Straighten the bobbins and use the first four downright pairs on the left to work the other side vein. This is started with the pinholes on the right, as described for the vein illustrated in fig. 42. When the pairs have been rolled back and tied between the bobbins of the resting downright pair, continue the main vein, using the runner pair that was left at 2. Make the second pair of side veins when these are reached, then continue ribbing the main vein and leaf stem.

After pins 5 and 6 (fig. 47), work to the plain side and, instead of using a turning stitch, top-sew the runners to the nearest hole of the large flower, then work back with them. Make a back stitch at 7, work to the plain side, top-sew the runners to 8, then work back to make up the back stitch at 7. Continue the rib up the side of the small leaf. This is made like the whole stitch leaves in the first pattern, laying back a pair from the rib at 9 and 10 and, after turning the top, hanging in a new pair at 11, 12 and 13, giving ten pairs altogether. Sew out into the flower, tie, bunch and cut off.

Set up again at 1, at the tip of the large leaf (fig. 49), with six pairs, a coarse pair and a magic thread. Work in whole stitch, adding a new pair at each of the ringed holes. After the edge stitch at 2, change to half stitch, i.e. work through the first pair in whole stitch, tie the runners (to keep the new pair in position), then work half stitch through the next two pairs, whole stitch with the pair after that, and sew the runners to the top hole of the middle vein, using the magic thread. Work back to 3, hang in a new pair, make the edge stitch and leave, after pushing these seven pairs well out of the way.

Find the first of the unworked downright pairs (sixth pair from left), sew it also to the top hole of the middle vein without removing the pin, then use it as runners to work in whole stitch to 4. Continue working this whole stitch half of the leaf, making edge stitches (and hanging in new pairs where indicated) on the left side, and top sewings into the centre vein on the right.

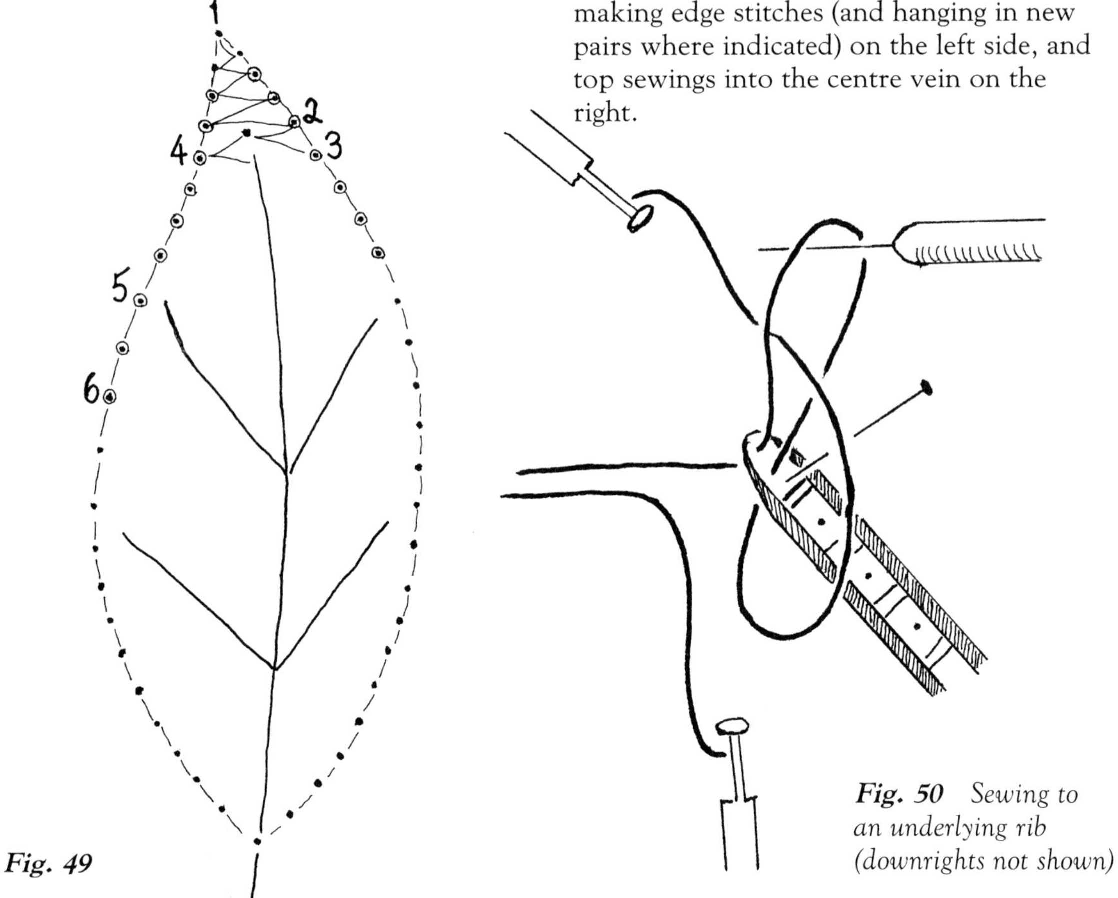

Fig. 49

Fig. 50 *Sewing to an underlying rib (downrights not shown)*

After 5, work back through three downright pairs, and sew the runners to the top hole of the side vein. This sewing, where the *runner* is attached to an underlying part and then continues to the end of the row, differs from previous sewings in that only one thread is used. Raise but do not remove the pin. Draw the leading runner thread through to form a loop, then pass the bobbin through its own loop (fig. 50). Leave the needle pin in the loop as you pull on the bobbin so that the knot does not tighten on itself until all the free thread has been pulled through. Return the bobbin to its place as leading runner and complete the row.

Do not allow any pins holding down the side vein to become trapped under the clothwork; remove them as you come to them and, after 6 (fig. 49), join once more, half-way down the side vein. As this join lies much closer to the right side, work the runners from 6 through until only three downright pairs remain unworked, then top-sew the leading thread to one of the side bars of the vein – choose one that is under the line being taken by the runners. Again pass the runner through its own loop, pull up and complete the row.

There are thirteen pairs in the section by now, and this should be sufficient, as the raised veins show up more clearly against a fairly thin clothwork. However, more pairs may be added if a denser texture is preferred. Continue working down the leaf, keeping level. Join to the tip of the next side vein, and again half-way down the vein, as the appropriate places are reached. Note that *these joins must not be done too soon*; the clothwork must have been worked almost past the place in which the join is to be made, otherwise the weaving will be distorted. Where in the row these joins are to be made is also a matter for the lacemaker's judgement – pull the downrights into vertical lines and this will show how many pairs must be worked through before the sewing can be made.

Reduce the number of pairs gradually as the leaf narrows, setting aside the last two pairs to be discarded on the pinhole side, and sew out, using top sewings, into one or two holes of the main rib at the end. When there is only one coarse thread, as here, lay this back and cut it off. Its partner may also be laid back and cut off, or it may be included in the bunch. Many lacemakers prefer to tie this single thread to a neighbouring thread that has already been sewn and tied, before including it in the bunch. Tie and bunch the threads and tie back the little bunch over the clothwork, using the discarded pairs that were set aside (fig. 22), having first trimmed short all other discarded pairs. Bow off the bobbins but do not trim off the ends until the rest of the leaf has been made – they can be pushed out of the way under a slider or cover cloth. This should leave the pinholes of the main rib clear for use again when the second half of the leaf is being made.

Return to the bobbins that were left at the division and work the half stitch part of the leaf, making top sewings into the main rib and adding new pairs until there are approximately ten pairs altogether. The joins into the side veins are done as before, using the leading runner thread for the sewing and passing the bobbin through its own loop. Then lay the bobbin down in its place as leading runner thread – do not twist it with its partner; the next stitch made with this pair will leave both pairs twisted. Gradually reduce the number of pairs and sew out into the main rib at the bottom of the leaf. This little bunch can also be tied back, though this is not really necessary as it can be made to lie over the whole stitch part.

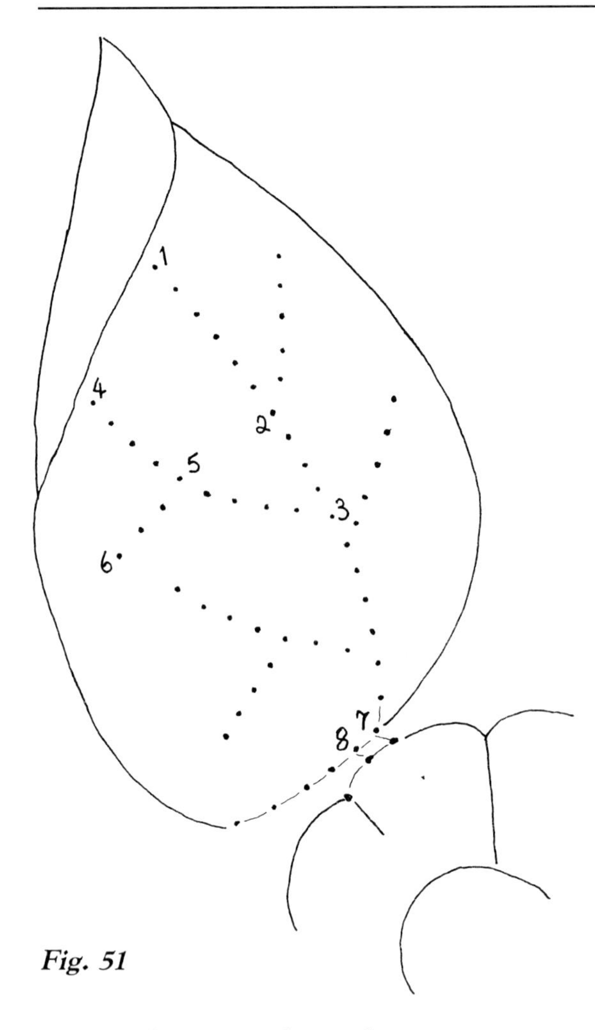

Fig. 51

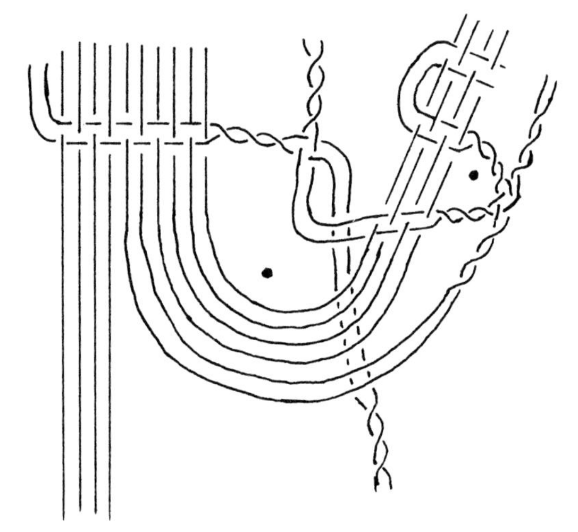

Fig. 52 Beginning a side vein on the pinhole side of a rib (no opposite side vein)

Leaf with staggered raised veins

Set up with seven pairs and a magic thread at 1 (fig. 51), and rib down, pinholes on the right, until the edge stitch at 2 has been made.

Single side vein on pinhole side of main vein

Leave the outer (edge) pair, lift the runners and the next three downright pairs over the edge pair, and use them to make the side vein. Give three twists to the left pair, which is to be the edge pair, untwist the right pair and use it as runners to work through two pairs to the left. Twist, set pin and make the edge stitch (fig. 52). Continue the side vein to the top and roll back as before. When the side vein is complete, lift all four pairs back over the edge pair of the main rib, and lay them between the bobbins of the nearest downright pair. Tie this pair twice over the bunch and place both bobbins of the tied pair to the left of the bunch and to the right of the remaining downright pair. Straighten out the bunched bobbins and choose the last pair on the right (next to the edge pair) as new runners. Work these through the downrights to the left, making the turning stitch and working back to the next pinhole of the main rib. If the bobbins are pulled up carefully, the plain side of the main rib should lie straight and unbroken past the side vein. Rib until the edge stitch at 3 has been made and leave.

Branching side vein

Make the side vein using the four downright pairs on the left, as shown in fig. 42, working to 4 and ignoring the branch. Roll back, using the method shown in fig. 43 as far as 5. When the winding pair has been

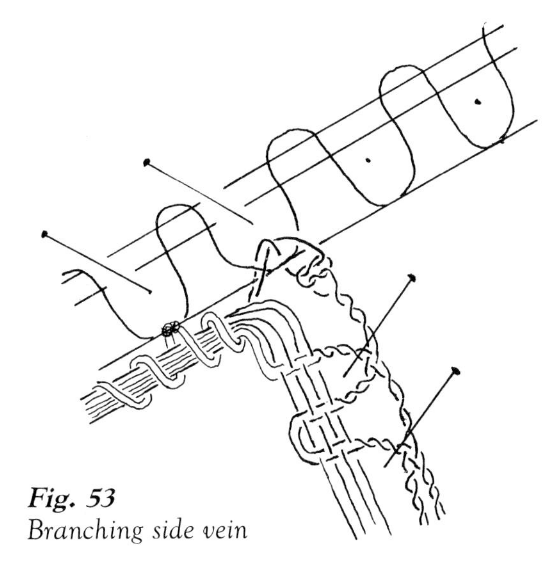

Fig. 53
Branching side vein

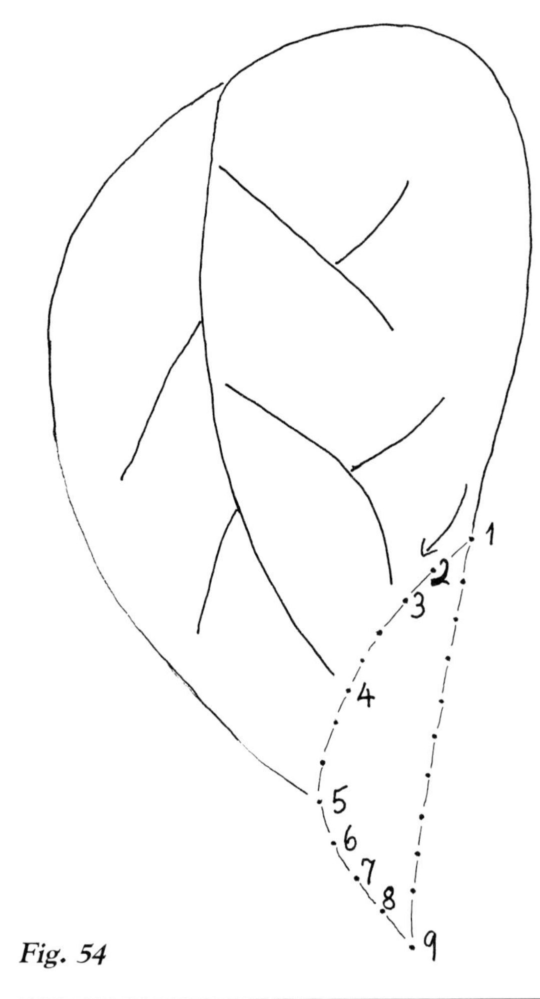

Fig. 54

sewn and tied here, use all four pairs to make the branch. Straighten the bobbins, give three twists to the tied pair and lay it on the right of the bunch as an edge pair. Use the outside left pair as runners and make the pinholes on the right (fig. 53). Rib to 6 and roll back, sewing into 5 again on the way back. Make sure that the knots after this sewing are firm and hold the roll close up against the rib. Then complete the roll to the mid-rib, tying up the four pairs between the bobbins of the resting downright pair, as before.

Make the remainder of the mid-rib and the side veins as above, continuing the rib along the base of the leaf. At 7 and 8 join to adjacent holes of the flower (*see* Glossary, *Sewing to Join Two Edges*), then rib up the outer side of the leaf.

After the edge stitch at 1 (fig. 54), change the side on which the pinholes are made (*see* fig. 15, p. 13), working the next pinhole at 2. At 3 join to the top hole of the adjacent side vein, and at 4 to the top of the mid-rib, using the magic thread. Hang in and lay back a new pair at 5, 6 and 7, and lay back a pair from the rib at 8. Work to 9, turn the pillow and work back in whole stitch, to fill the turned tip of the leaf.

After the sewing at 4, take the second and third downright threads from the right and lay them back. Throw out one pair similarly at every subsequent hole on the rib side. Keep these pairs in order, as they will be brought in again for the half stitch, filling the left part of the leaf. After the sewing at 2, throw out a pair on both sides, which should leave four pairs. Work the sewn pair through the two downright pairs and top-sew this and also the edge pair to the upper bar of 1. Tie all four pairs three times, then cross the two sewn pairs under, and tie them three times over, the downright pairs. One of these pairs can be left for the half stitch filling; the other three are bowed off,

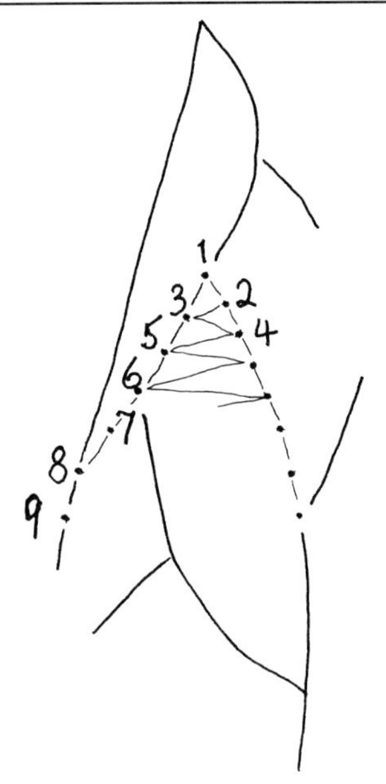

Fig. 55

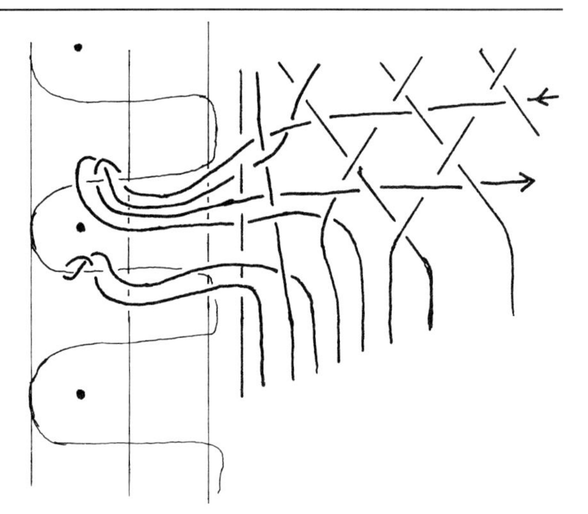

Fig. 56 *Adding a new pair to half stitch along a sewing edge*

but not trimmed short until the filling has been made.

Sew in a new pair at 1, 2 and 3 (fig. 55), using top sewings. Bring down the first pair to be discarded in the whole stitch section, laying it between the pairs hanging from 1 and 3. Use the pair from 2 as runners, working a whole stitch with the pair from 1, a half stitch with the next pair, and a whole stitch with the pair from 3. Leave the runners. Tie the pair from 3 once and use it as runners to work a half stitch and a whole stitch with the two pairs on its right. *Sew the runners at 4 and leave. Bring down the next of the discarded pairs to lie next to the abandoned runners on the other side, and also sew in a new pair at 5 to lie as the outer pair on the left. Work the runners from 4 to 5 in half stitch, but making a whole stitch with the first and last pairs. Leave the runners, tie the last pair they came through once and use it as runners to work in half stitch to the next hole on the other side, making a whole stitch with the last pair. Repeat from *, bringing down a discarded pair and also sewing in a new pair at each of 6 and 7.

Bring down the last discarded pair, and from now on work through the outer pair in whole stitch at both ends of every row. There should be twelve pairs in all at this stage. It is not necessary to sew into 8, as it is so close to 7 – sew into 9 instead. Continue the filling, joining into the tips, and also once or twice along the side veins and branches, as in the last leaf.

Gradually add four more pairs on the outer (left) side – this is best done when the runners are on the inner (vein) side. Sew the new pair round the lower bar of the same outer hole into which the runners were last sewn. Lay the new pair between the bobbins of the whole stitch pair, then twist the inner bobbin of the new pair once with the next bobbin on its right (fig. 56). Work the runners from the inner side through the row and sew them into the next outer hole.

Near the end of the leaf, begin to slope by sewing twice into the mid-rib holes. Arrange the work so that from a sewing round the upper bar of hole 1 (fig. 57), the runners can work through to be sewn to the left bar of 2. There should be fourteen pairs left at this stage, one pair having been removed on the left in each of the two previous rows.

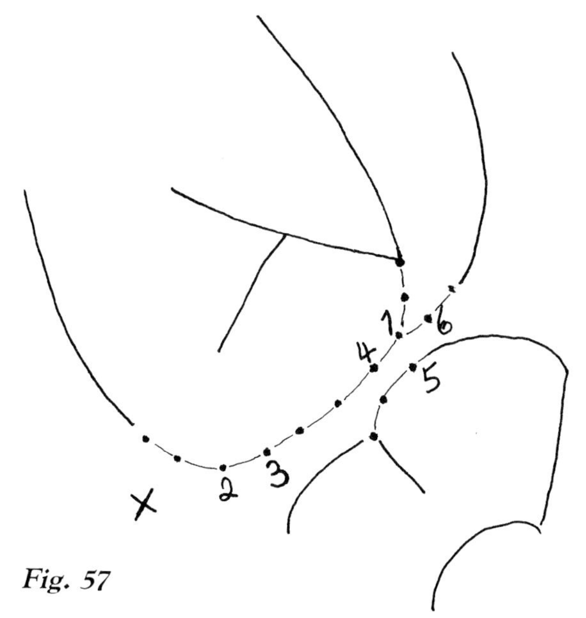

Fig. 57

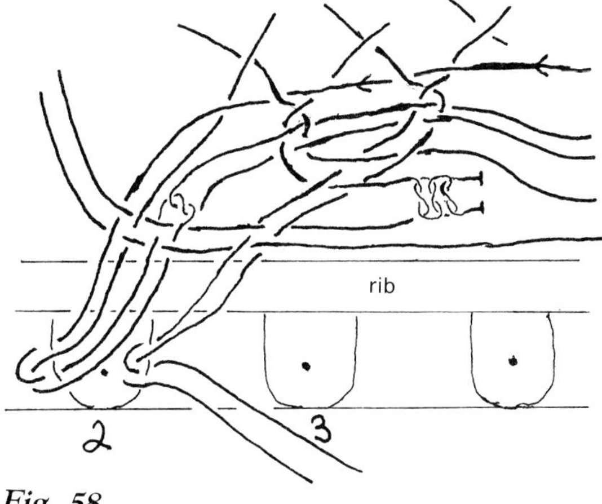

Fig. 58

Change to whole stitch. Work the sewn runners from 2 through the first downright pair, tie them once, then work them through two more pairs and leave them. Take the last pair the runners passed through as new runners, work them back through two pairs, and sew them into the right bar of 2. *Take the second and third downright threads, i.e. the fourth and fifth from the left, counting the runners. Tie these three times and lay them back (fig. 58). Work the sewn runners through three pairs to the right and leave them. Use the last pair they passed through as new runners, working them back through two pairs and sewing them into the left bar of 3. Repeat from *, using both bars of each hole and taking out one pair after each sewing, until the second sewing at 4 (fig. 57) has been done, then work the runners through the remaining four pairs and sew them into the lower bar of 1.

Sew the outer left downright pair to 5 (edge sewing) and twist it three times – it will be the edge pair for the whole stitch half of the leaf. Take any other two downright bobbins, tie them three times and lay one of them to the back, so that there is an uneven number of bobbins left. Take a bobbin wound with coarse thread, tie its end to a pin set at approximately X, and lay the bobbin in position to the right of the twisted pair from 5.

Work the whole stitch part of the leaf, beginning with the sewn runners from 1 and setting the first pin at 6. Hang in a new pair here and at every subsequent outer hole until there are twelve pairs altogether. Tidy up the half stitch part of the leaf, trimming off all the discarded pairs, when the first row or two have been worked. Join twice into each side vein when passing, as before.

Near the top, make one or two back stitches, arranging the rows so that from 1 (fig. 59) the runners travel to 2. After the sewing here, work back through one pair, tie the runners and continue to 3, where a back stitch is begun. Before returning, sew the first downright pair on the right round the lower bar of 2, tie it three times and lay it back. Sew the next downright pair to the upper bar of 4, tie it three times and lay it back. Work the runners from 3 through the downrights, sew them also to the upper bar of 4, and work back to 3 to make up the back stitch. Sew the outer downright pair on the right to the lower bar of 4, tie it

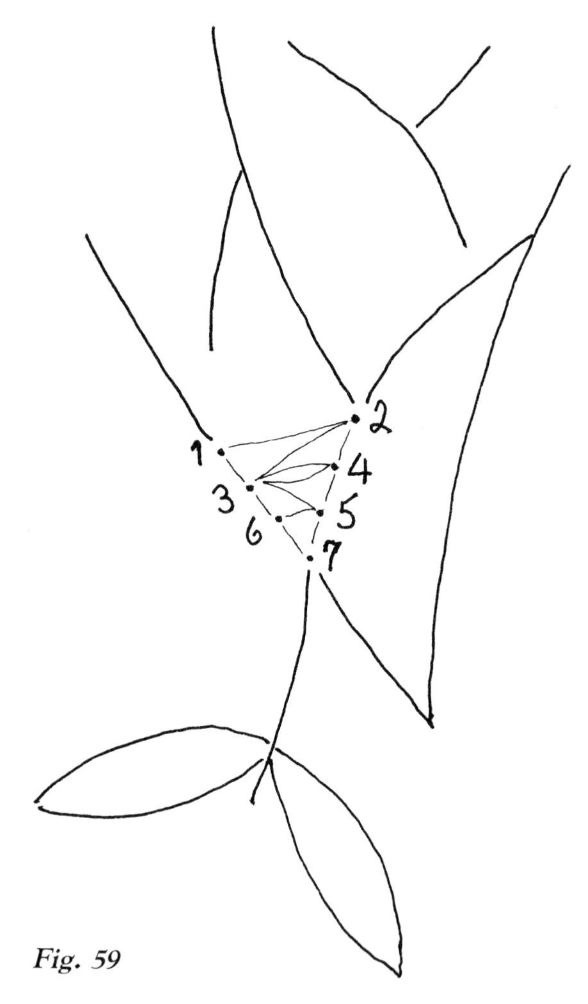

Fig. 59

three times and lay it back. Sew the next downright pair round the upper bar of 5, tie it three times and lay it back. Work the runners from 3 through the downrights, sew them also to the upper bar of 5, work back to 6 and make the edge stitch. Sew the outer downright pair on the right to the upper bar of 7, tie it once and leave it. Work the runners from 6 through the downrights, sew them also to the upper bar of 7, tie them once and leave them. Replace pin 7. Lift all the downright pairs and lay them to the right of pin 7. Remove pin 7 again, sew the edge pair to this hole with an edge sewing, tie it once and twist it three times. Replace pin 7.

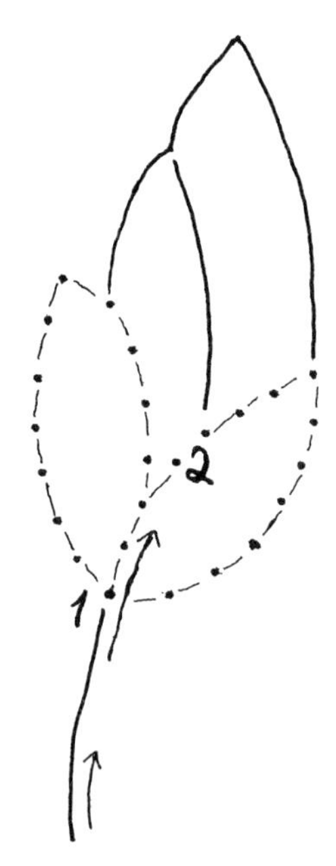

Fig. 60

Lay back one of the downright bobbins, weave the coarse thread under and over through the remaining four downright pairs to the right, and leave it to be cut off. Now lift the four downright pairs, and also the two pairs sewn to the upper bar of 7, back over pin 7, laying them down to the left of the twisted pair. These seven pairs now make the rib leading to the bud. Keeping pinholes on the right, begin with the pair next to the twisted (edge) pair as runners, and work them first to the plain side.

Follow the direction of the arrows in fig. 60, working into the sepal of the bud, which is made like the leaves in the first pattern. Lay back a pair from the rib at each of the last two holes before the point, turn, and hang in two new pairs on the pinhole side when working back. Reduce to seven pairs again and, after the sewing at 1, tie the sewn pair twice, place the other six pairs between the tied bobbins, and tie these twice again over the bunch. Make a short roll to 2, then rib up to the point of the other sepal, laying out a pair from the rib at each of the last three holes before the point. After turning,

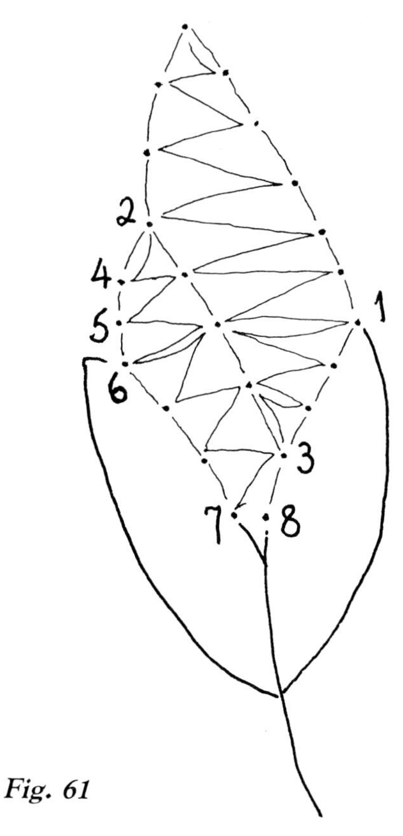

Fig. 61

hang in one new pair on the pinhole side. Complete the sepal and sew out at the bottom.

Sew in six pairs (two sewings) at 1 (fig. 61), and rib up to the point of the petal, laying back a pair from the rib at each of the last two holes before the point. Turn, and work back in half stitch, remembering to tie the runners at 2 and also after the top sewing at 1. Make two back stitches near the end so that, from the last pinhole, the runners can work through to 3. Roll all six pairs back to 2; sew the pair that attaches the roll to this hole too, then use it as a runner pair to work in half stitch to 4, where it makes the edge stitch with the other sewn pair from 2. Tie the runners after the edge stitch at 5. Sew out the edge pair at 6 and, after sewing the runners at 6, take out a pair on the left side. Continue with the remaining four pairs to the end of the petal. After sewing at

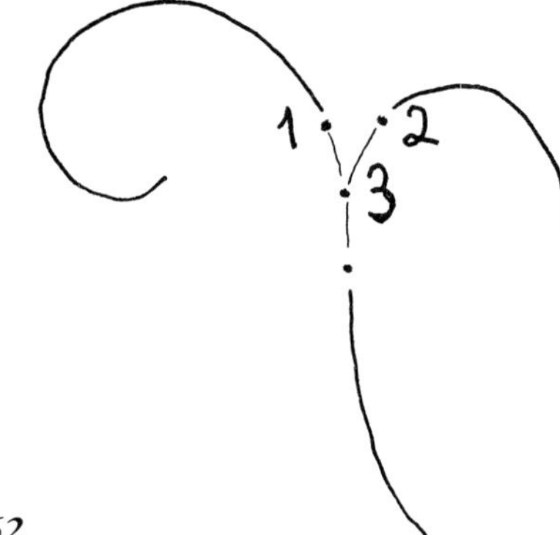

Fig. 62

7, work one more row in whole stitch and sew out – the runners to the lower bar of 3, and the middle downright pair to the upper bar of 8. (No need to sew the other two pairs.) Tie all four pairs three times. Cut off.

The tendril that ends in this bud is started at both tips, with five pairs in each. After the edge stitches have been made at 1 and 2 (fig. 62), lay both sets side by side. Work the runner pair from 1 through the downrights to its left, make a turning stitch at the end of the row, and work back through all pairs of both sets. Twist the runners once and leave them. The last pair the runners passed will be the new runners, but before returning with them, take a downright pair out of each set and lay them back. In addition, give three twists to the last pair on the left. Work the new runners towards 3, where the next edge stitch is made with the twisted pair. Work another row of rib, then discard another downright pair. Complete the rib with the seven pairs remaining, and sew out into the bud.

The pairs of leaves above and below the bud are made like the leaves in the first pattern, using seven pairs for the ribs and adding one to three pairs for working back.

Backward-facing flower

Begin with the stem, top-sewing seven pairs into the stem of the leaf with raised veins,

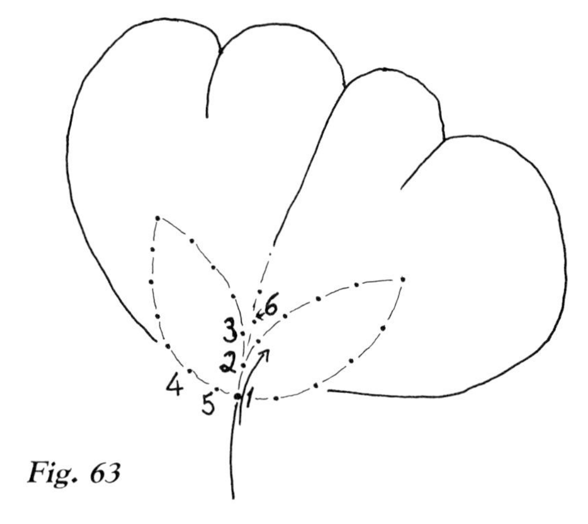

Fig. 63

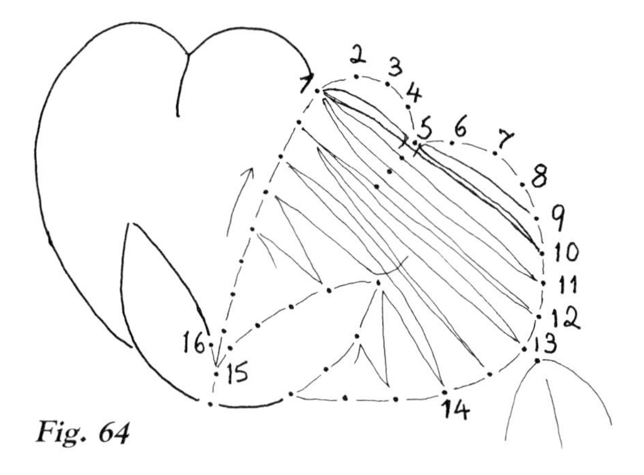

Fig. 64

and working in rib, pinholes on the right. After the third pin *work to the plain side, top-sew the runners to the nearest hole on the side of the leaf, work them back again to the pinhole side and make the next edge stitch. Repeat from * twice more, then continue the rib into the left sepal. This is made like the sepal in the last bud. At the end, when the runners have been sewn at 1 (fig. 63), tie them twice, lay the remaining six pairs between the tied bobbins, and tie these twice again over the bunch. Wind the tied pair once round the bunch, sew it in at 2, tie it twice, twist it once and leave it to become an edge pair. Choose a pair from the bunch as runners, work this through the other pairs to 3 and make the edge stitch with the twisted pair. Continue the rib to the top of the second sepal and work back as before. After pins 4 and 5, lay back a pair on the right-hand side; these will be used again. Complete the sepal, discarding one more pair (to be cut off later) before sewing out the remaining five pairs. Bunch these pairs but do not cut them off.

Sew the first pair that was laid back to 3, tie it once and twist it once or twice, making it an edge pair. Sew the next of the laid-back pairs to 2, and tie it twice. Turn back the bunched pairs, lay them between the tied pair at 2, and tie this twice again over the bunch. Choose a pair from the bunch to be runners, and work these through the other pairs to 6, where the edge stitch is made with the pair hanging from 3. Continue the rib up the side of the petal.

At 1 (fig. 64) hang in and lay back a pair after the edge stitch has been made. Work through the first pair, tie the runners and continue the rib along the top of the petal, hanging in and laying back one pair at 2, two pairs at 3 and one pair each at 4 and 5. Having made the edge stitch at 5, leave, and use the four inner pairs to make the little indentation, as in the large flower. Before continuing the rib, hang in and lay back another new pair at 5 (hanging it over the runners, second pair from edge). Lay back a pair from the rib at 6, 7 and 8. Rib to 9, make the edge stitch and turn the pillow.

Work the runners through the first downright pair, tie them, then work them in half stitch through the next four pairs and make a whole stitch with the pair after that (hanging from 5). Tie this pair once, making sure that the knot sits well up, and use it to work in half stitch to 10, making a whole stitch with the last downright pair. Hang in a new pair before making the edge stitch at 10. This pair is laid inside the first downright thread in the usual way, its inner bobbin twisted with the next bobbin on the left. Leave.

Using the pair from 1 as runners, work it in half stitch through five pairs to the right, making a whole stitch with the first and last pairs. Tie the last pair the runners passed through well up, lay it down to the left of the runners and leave it. (This row is made to fill in the lip of the petal.)

Bring the runners from 10 through all pairs in half stitch, making a whole stitch with the first and last pairs. Top-sew the runners to the upper bar of 1. Continue working in half stitch, hanging in a new pair at 11, 12 and 13 (giving eighteen pairs altogether). On the other side, use hole 1 once more and also sew twice into the next hole below it. After the first sewing into the hole below 1, work back through six pairs, sew the leading runner thread to the end hole of the indentation (fig. 50), and continue the row. At 13 join to the top hole of the adjacent leaf, using the magic thread (*see* Glossary). Leave the runners temporarily at 14; the work now divides, each part being made separately on either side of the sepal.

Not counting the runners and edge pair at 14, take the sixth downright pair from the right, sew it to the top hole of the sepal and use it as a runner pair to work in half stitch to the left, making a whole stitch with the first and last pairs. Continue this section, top-sewing on both sides and reducing to seven pairs. After the last sewing at 15, tie the runners twice and leave them. Sew the outer downright pair on the left to 16 and tie it twice. Lay the remaining five pairs between the bobbins of this sewn pair and tie it again twice over the bunch. Use this pair as a winding pair to make a roll to 1. Use the sewn pair from 15 to attach the roll to the side of the petal, making the last sewing at 1 with this pair also. Leave these pairs on one side. Bow off, and trim short all discarded pairs.

Return to the unworked part of the petal – the runners were left at 14 – and complete this section, making the first top sewing into the top hole of the sepal. Reduce the number of pairs until there are only four pairs left in the last row, and sew out into the side of the sepal. Bunch and cut off.

Disentangle the pairs left hanging at 1 (fig. 65). Use them to rib along the top of the

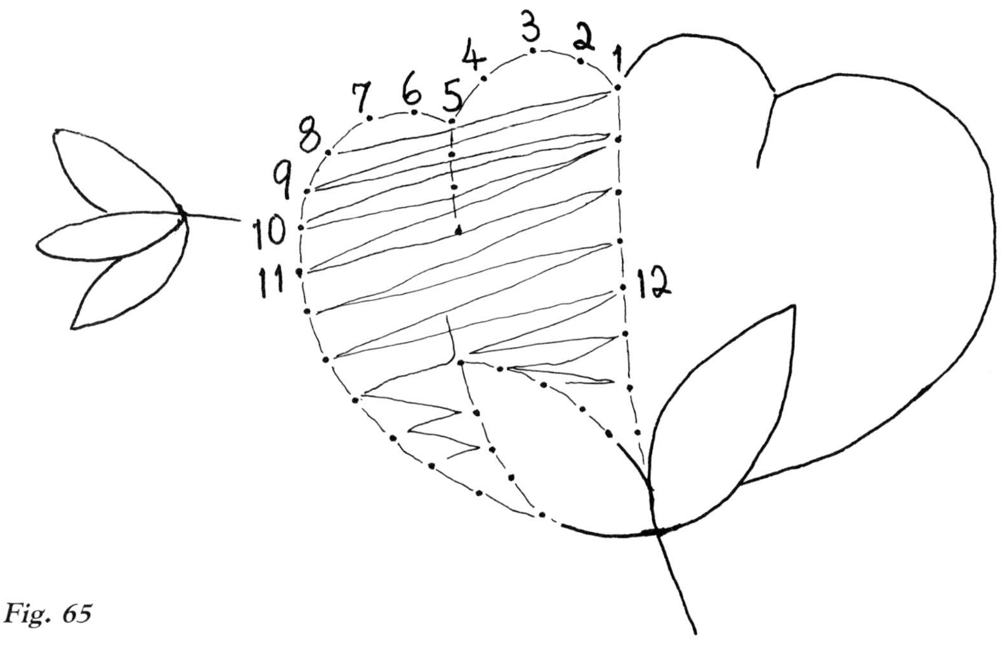

Fig. 65

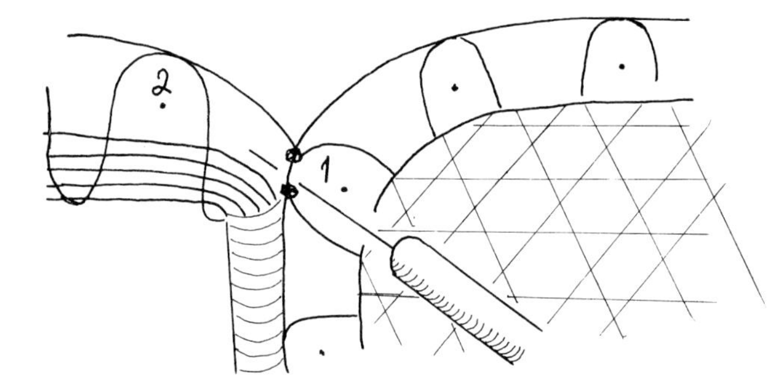

Fig. 66

other petal, hanging in and laying back one new pair at 2, two pairs at 3, one pair at 4 and two pairs at 5, one before and one after making the little side vein (pinholes on the left). At 6 and 7 lay back a pair from the rib, work to 8, turn the pillow and leave.

To fill in the first lip of the petal, take the pair hanging from 2 in half stitch through three pairs, in whole stitch through the next pair, and leave it to become passive. Tie the last pair passed through, and work back with it in half stitch through two pairs and in whole stitch through the last pair. Sew it at 1, as shown in fig. 66. Leave the sewn pair to become the outer downright pair on this side.

Work across the petal with the runners from 8, tying them at the beginning of the row and sewing them to the lower side bar of 1 at the end. Continue working in half stitch, hanging in a new pair at 9, 10 and 11 (making sixteen pairs altogether) and, on the other side, sewing twice into the hole below 1. When passing the last hole of the underlying rib, join as before.

Leave the runners when they have been sewn at 12 and divide the work, taking the seventh downright pair from the right (not counting the runners), sewing it to the top hole of the sepal, and using it as runners to work the section on the left of the sepal. Reduce to a very few pairs and sew out into the side of the sepal. Tie, bunch and cut off.

Before working the section on the right of the sepal, take the outermost downright thread on the left and sew it to the top hole of the sepal, putting the bobbin through its own loop (fig. 50). Pull up carefully and lay this thread down again beside its partner. (The purpose of this sewing is to prevent a hole forming in the half stitch, which would otherwise be caused by the change of direction of this thread.) The sewn runners at 12 continue this section, the first sewing being made into the top of the sepal. After sewing out, the pairs are tied and cut off – they do not need to be bunched.

The single leaf on the stem of this flower is raised along the lower edge and is made like the leaves in the first pattern, using ten pairs at the widest part.

To make the bud above this flower, sew seven pairs for the stem into holes 10 and 11 (fig. 65), and rib, pinholes on the left,

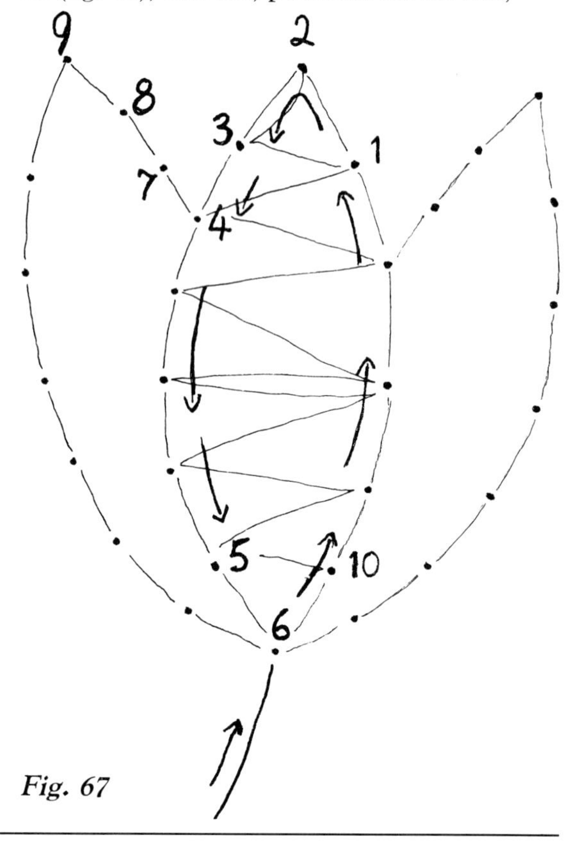

Fig. 67

into and right round the middle sepal, following the direction of the arrows in fig. 67. Hang in and lay back two pairs each at 1, 2 and 3, and one new pair at 4 (remember to tie the runners after 2). Push the new pairs well out of the way and complete the rib to 5. Work to the plain side, top-sew the runners to the upper bar of 6, tie them twice, lay the other six pairs between them, and tie them twice again over the bunch. Replace pin 6 to the right of the bunch. Use these pairs to make a roll to 4, sewing both the winding pair and the attaching pair to this hole, then rib to 9, laying back a pair from the rib at 7 and 8. Turn, and work back down the side sepal, making a plain edge on the outer side and top sewings on the inner side once the two laid-back pairs have been used. Reduce to four pairs at the end, saving the last two discarded pairs on the outer side for tying back the bunch. Sew out the runners and edge pair, one to each side bar of 6. Tie, bunch, turn back the little bunch and tie it down with the reserved pairs. Bow off but do not trim the ends until the other sepals have been made. Replace pin 6.

Return to the pairs that were hung in at the top of the middle sepal, and lay these straight, raising pins 1, 2 and 3 to check that no threads have accidentally become hooked round them. Use one of the pairs hanging from 2 as runners, and fill in the sepal, taking in the other pairs as you come to them and then making top sewings on both sides. Do not discard any pairs. After sewing at 10, tie the runners twice, place the other pairs between them and tie them twice over the bunch. Make a roll up the side, then rib up to the point of the last sepal and complete this in the same way as the one on the other side. Sew out, bunch and cut off.

Sew in seven pairs, using holes 1 and 2 (fig. 68), and rib up the line between the

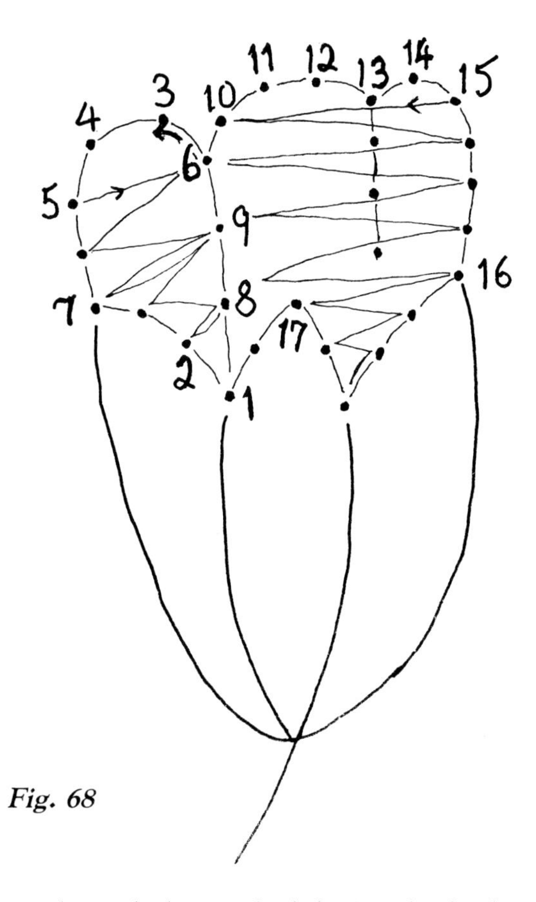

Fig. 68

petals, pinholes on the left. At 3 lay back a pair from the rib and tie the runners when they have passed back through the first downright pair. Rib to 4, lay back another pair from the rib, work to 5 and turn the pillow. Work back in half stitch, following the course of the runners shown on the diagram. Sew out the edge pair at 7, tie it three times and lay it back. The runners are top-sewn into this hole and tied, when they have passed back through the first pair.

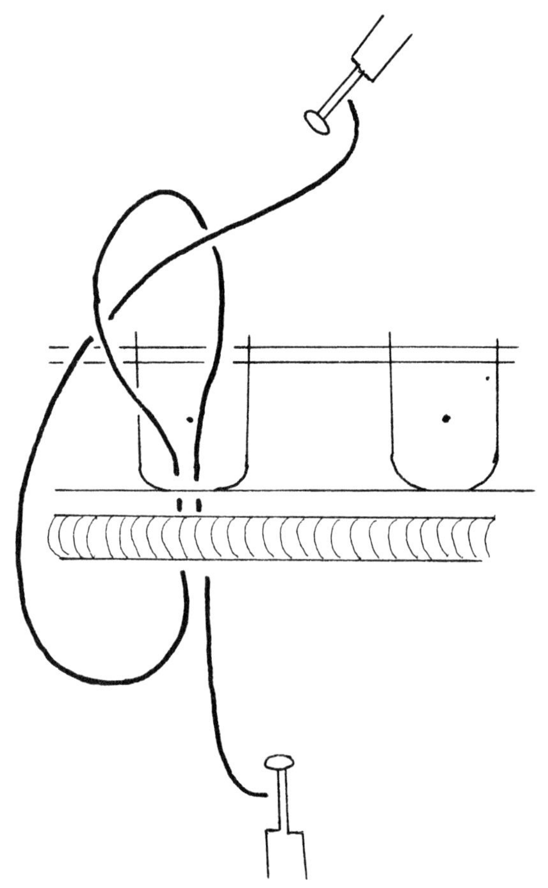

Fig. 69 *Sewing in a new pair round a roll*

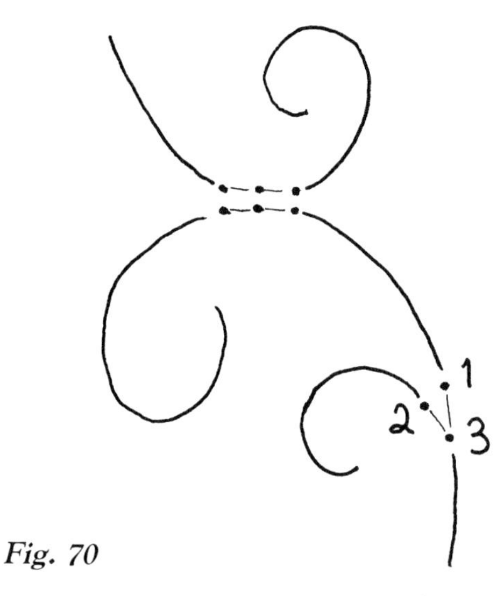

Fig. 70

After the second sewing at 8, tie the sewn pair, place the remaining five pairs between these bobbins, and tie them again over the bunch. Then wind the tied pair round the bunch to make a roll to 3, where the winding pair is sewn in, tied twice, twisted, and left to become an edge pair. To attach the roll, sew in a new pair at 9 (fig. 69), tie it once, sew it round the roll as usual to 6, and tie it twice.

The seven pairs now rib along the top of the larger petal, beginning with the tied pair from 6 as runners. Hang in and lay back a new pair at 10, 11, 12 and 13. Make the little side vein, rib to 14 and lay back a pair from the rib. Rib to 15 and turn the pillow. Fill in the petal with half stitch, following the course shown for the runners on the diagram and remembering to join the leading runner thread to the last hole of the little side vein at the appropriate place. Sew out the edge pair at 16 and tie it three times. After top-sewing the runners at 16, leave them and sew out the second and third downright threads from the left to 17. Tie these two threads three times and lay them back, leaving the two odd bobbins to make the whole stitch pair on the left. Continue with the runners from 16, discarding pairs on both sides to leave only three or four pairs to be sewn out at the end. These are bowed off after tying and do not need to be bunched.

The rib tendrils are made as before, with five pairs in each branch. The longer branch is joined to the tendril on the other side at three holes where they run parallel (*see* Glossary, *Sewing to Join Two Edges*). Leave the longer tendril when the edge stitch at 1 (fig. 70) has been made. Make the shorter tendril as far as 2, then work the runners to the plain side and leave them. Remove a downright pair from this set. Lay both sets side by side. Work the runners from 1 through both sets and make the turning stitch but, before returning, discard a pair

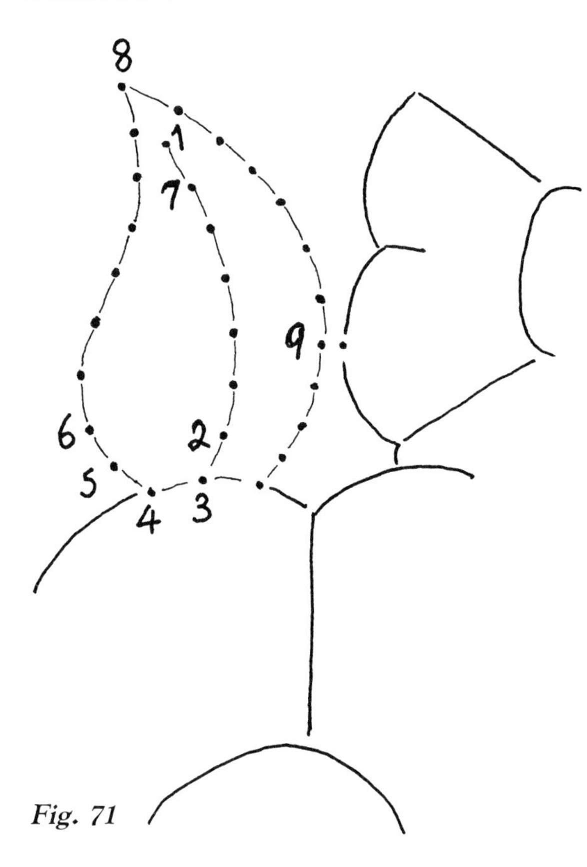

Fig. 71

from the right set. Work the runners back through both sets to 3, where the next edge stitch is made, and continue the rib, discarding another pair in the next row. Sew out into the bud.

The seven pairs needed for the short piece of stem are sewn into the side of the backward-facing flower. Rib down with pinholes on the right, and sew out into the leaf with raised veins.

The small whole stitch leaf which joins into the large flower has a raised vein down the middle. Hang seven pairs and a magic thread round pin 1 (fig. 71) and rib down the vein, pinholes on the right. After the edge stitch at 2, lay back a pair from the rib. Work the runners to the plain side, make the turning stitch and leave them. Sew the edge pair from 2 with an edge sewing to 3, tie it once and lay it to the back next to the pair already there. Work the runners from the plain side through the downrights and sew them to 3. Lay back another pair from the rib. Work the sewn runners through the first downright pair, tie them once, work through the remaining two downright pairs, make the turning stitch, work back and sew the runners at 4. Lay back a pair from the rib. Work another row of rib, tying the runners when they have passed through the first of the two remaining downright pairs. On returning, sew the runners once more to 4. Tie the runners once, twist them three times and leave them to become an edge pair. Turn the pillow.

Take the second pair from the left (i.e. the old edge pair which was sewn at 3 and laid back) as runners, and work them through four pairs to the right. Twist them, set pin 5 under them, hang in a new pair and make the edge stitch. Work back through all pairs, including the pair that was laid back at 2. This pair becomes the new runner pair, after it has been tied, and works back to the pinhole side. Continue normally, making top sewings on the left and pinholes on the right. Tie the runners at 6. Discard three pairs gradually as the leaf narrows, and sew twice into hole 7 to begin the turn round the top of the leaf. Use the magic thread for the first sewing at 1, and thereafter sew into this hole without removing the pin (or, if this is too difficult, remove the pin but use a threaded needle to do the sewing) until the tip has been turned and the weaving is level again; it will take approximately three sewings at 1. Remember to tie the runners at 8. Work the other half of the leaf, top-sewing into the middle vein and adding three pairs as the braid widens. At 9 join to the nearest hole of the flower. Reduce to five or six pairs at the end, and sew out into the flower. After bunching, the pairs can either be bowed off and trimmed short or, if preferred, the bunch may be tied back using two of the discarded pairs.

The butterfly

This can also be used on its own as a motif for a key-ring or brooch. Begin with the feelers: sew two pairs at 1 on the large flower (fig. 72) and make a half stitch plait to reach the head. To make the other feeler set a pin at 2, hang two pairs open round it (i.e. one bobbin of each pair on each side of the pin), twist both 'pairs' three times and work the half stitch plait as far as the head. Set pin 3 between the pairs of one plait and lay the pairs of the other plait round the same pin, together with two new pairs (fig. 73). Twist all 'pairs' twice, add a coarse pair and proceed as usual when starting at a point, working first towards the right. Hang in a new pair at 4 and 5 (tying the runners after each of these pins), and at 6 join to the opposite hole of the flower petal. Work down the body, making a vein down the middle if desired. Ladder trail was used in the worked sample, and another pair was added in order to give an equal number of

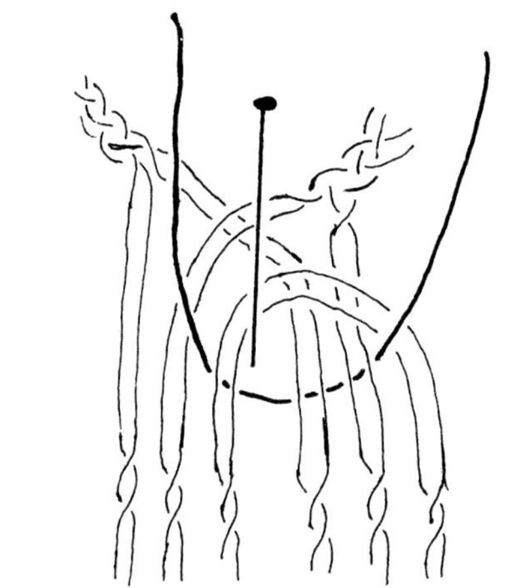

Fig. 73

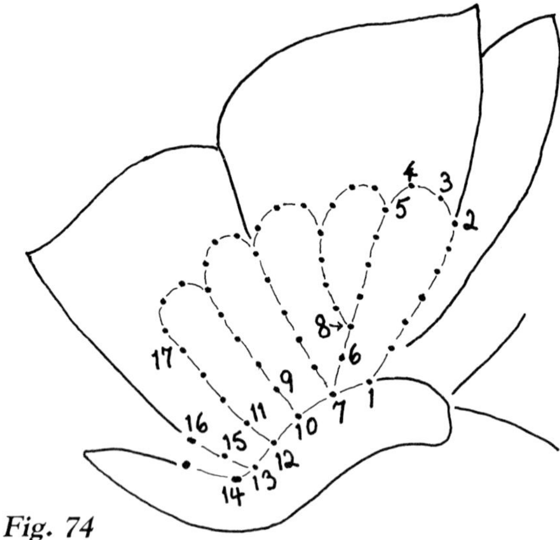

Fig. 74

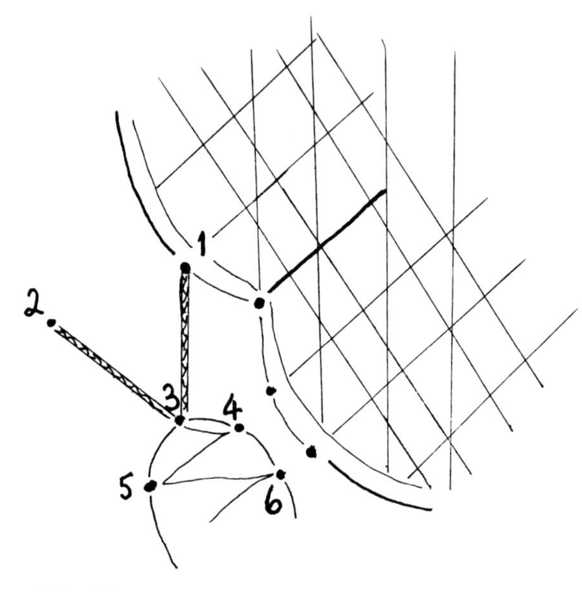

Fig. 72

downrights on each side. Join again to the petal lower down the body, where the two lines of holes run parallel. Finish as normal at the point, tying back the little bunch of threads over the body.

The raised taps forming the inside of both wings are made next. Sew in six pairs at 1 (fig. 74) and rib up the side of the first tap. Hang in and lay back a new pair at 2. At 3 hang in and lay back a new pair, and also lay back a pair from the rib. Rib to 4 and turn the pillow. Work down the tap as usual, hanging in a new pair at 5 and making one or two back stitches so that, at the end, the runners can work from 6 to 7, where they are sewn to the right bar of the hole. By this time the number of pairs should have been reduced to six again. Roll up to 5.

All the other taps are made with eight pairs, reducing at the bottom to six pairs to make the roll and rib. The next tap finishes at 8 on the side of the first tap. Save one of the discarded pairs to fill in the gap here when the third tap is being made. This tap also finishes at 7, the runners being sewn round the left bar of the hole.

At 9 on the fourth tap begin a back stitch (there should still be seven pairs in use at this stage), work back and sew the runners to the left bar of 7. Work the sewn runners back through one pair, tie them once, then work them through two more pairs and leave them. Take the last downright pair the runners passed through. Use these as new runners to work through two pairs to the right, and sew them to the right bar of 10. Lay back the second and third downright threads from the right (these can be cut off later and do not need to be tied). Work the sewn runners through all downright pairs and make up the back stitch at 9. Work back again, sew the runners to the left bar of 10, tie them twice, lay all other bobbins between them, and tie them twice again over the bunch. Roll to the top of the last tap. At the end of this tap the threads have to be turned so that they can be used to outline the wings.

From a back stitch begun at 11, work to the other side, sew the runners to the left bar of 10, work back through one pair, tie the runners once, work through two more pairs, and leave the runners. Take the last downright pair the runners passed through, and use these as new runners to work through two pairs to the right, sewing them to the left bar of 12. Lay back the second and third downright threads from the right. Work the sewn runners from 12 through three pairs to the left, leave them, and use the last pair they worked through to return through two pairs to the right. Sew the runners to the left bar of 13. Work back through all downright pairs and make up the back stitch at 11. Return through all pairs, sew the runners with an edge sewing to 14, tie them once, twist them twice, and leave them to become an edge pair. Turn the pillow.

Untwist the edge pair at 11 and use it as runners to work to 15, making the edge stitch with the twisted pair from 14. Continue the rib, hanging in a new pair or pairs on the pinhole side until there are seven pairs altogether (also join to the body of the butterfly at 16). Top-sew the runners when they are on the plain side to the opposite holes of the last tap. The last of these sewings is at 17 – after this the rib goes on independently, with turning stitches on the plain side. Remember to tie the runners at points where the rib makes a sharp turn. The line between the back and front wings is made in the same way as the lines between petals in the flowers, i.e. rib down to the taps, join, then roll back and continue the rib round the edge of the front wing.

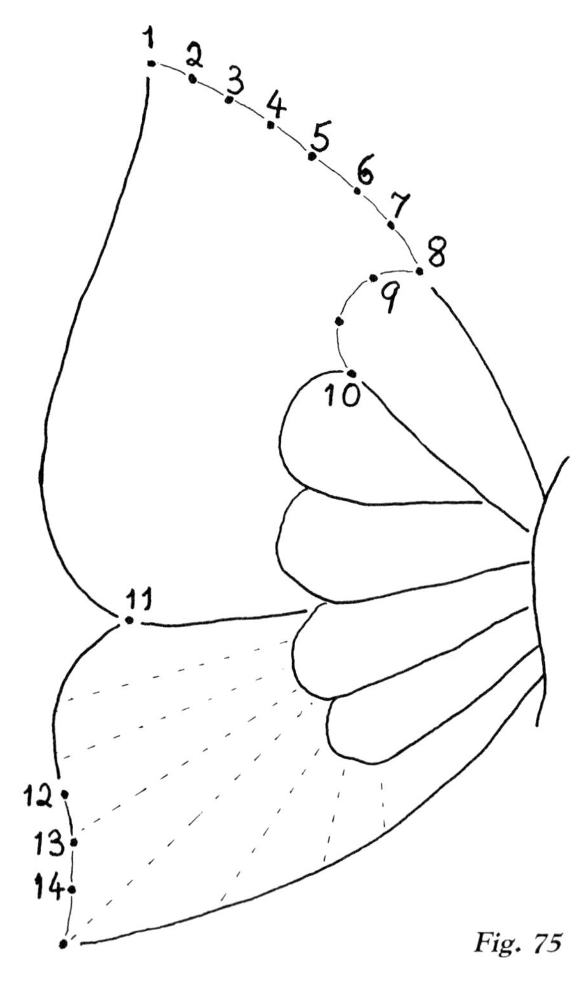

Fig. 75

Hang in and lay back a new pair at 1 and 2 (fig. 75), two new pairs at 3, one at 4, two at 5. At 6 and 7 lay back a pair from the rib. Work one more row of rib, then sew out the edge pair and runners at 8 and tie them three times. Tie the next two downright pairs three times. Sew the next downright pair (the last one on the left) to 8. Lay this pair to the back, next to the pair from 7. Place the two tied downright pairs between the sewn runners and edge pair, and tie these three times over the bunch. Lift up the bunch and replace pin 8 to the right of it. Bow off the bunched bobbins, but do not trim the ends short until the butterfly has been completed.

Turn the pillow so that the ten pairs that were laid back are in front of you. The pair that was sewn at 8 and laid back is the runner pair. Work it in half stitch through seven pairs to the left, making a whole stitch with the first and last pairs. Leave the runners, tie the last pair they passed through once, and work back with it in half stitch, making a whole stitch with the last pair. Top-sew the runners at 9 and work back through all pairs. Leave the runners, tie the last pair they passed through (the pair from 1), and work back with this to the other side, sewing to 9 a second time. Continue filling in the front wing, making top sewings on both sides. Do not miss the holes from which the taps diverge (such as 10), and tie the runners at these places after they have been sewn and returned through the first pair.

In the last row before crossing into the hind wing, discard a pair on the inner side and sew in a new pair at 11 (as described in the leaf with staggered veins, fig. 56). Join one of the central downright pairs to the rib between the wings, as described for the large flower. In the next two rows remove a pair from the right side (there should now be eight pairs remaining). At the same time begin to slope by sewing twice into most of the holes on the right; the direction of the weaving should gradually veer round, as shown by the dotted lines in fig. 75.

Sew in a new pair at 12, 13 and 14, and at the same time discard a pair on the inner side in each of these rows, so that the number of pairs does not alter. This procedure prevents distortion in the weaving, which might otherwise occur due to the extended outer corner. Once the outer corner has been passed, continue to reduce on the inner side, leaving only three or four pairs to be sewn out into the side of the lowest tap.

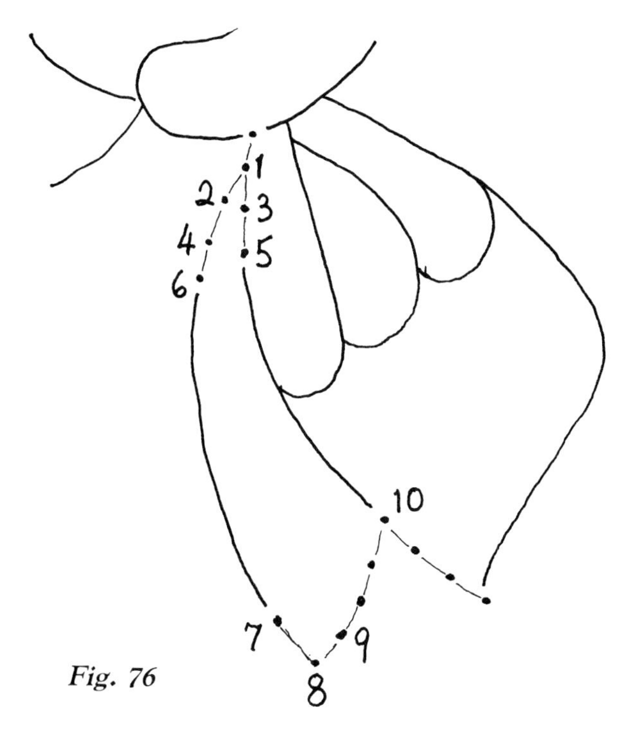

Fig. 76

For the fragment of the other forewing, sew in three pairs at 1 (fig. 76). Twist the outer left pair three times; this is to be the edge pair. Make a whole stitch with the other two pairs, twist the left of these three times and set pin 2 under it. Before making the edge stitch, hang in a new pair, laying it down between the bobbins of the one downright pair. *After the edge stitch, work back and top-sew the runners at 3. Work to 4 and hang in a new pair. Repeat from * once more, using holes 5 and 6. Continue in rib with these six pairs. At 7 lay back a pair from the rib, rib to 8, tie the runners after this hole, then rib to 9.

Turn the pillow (if you have not already done so) and change to half stitch, taking in the pair left out from 7 at the end of the row, tying it, and using it as the new runner pair in the normal way. Continue in half stitch, making top sewings on the right and edge stitches on the left. After the last of these, work to the other side and, before returning, top-sew the edge pair to the upper bar of 10. Tie this three times and lay it back to be cut off later. On return, the runners are sewn to the lower bar of 10 and tied when they have come back through the first downright pair. Continue to fill in the wing with these five pairs, top-sewing on both sides (twice into the next hole in the right, to keep level) and removing one more pair, where the wing becomes very narrow, before sewing out.

Working Methods

Alternative way of making a roll

The method used in the indentations of the flower petals – making and attaching the roll at the same time, using only the winding pair for the whole operation – is as common as that described in pattern 2, 'Rosette'. Both are correct and produce much the same appearance. Note that, when using the winding pair to attach the roll, two knots are necessary after each sewing. If only one were made, it would very easily pull away from the edge when the winding pair makes the couple of turns round the roll before the next sewing.

Raised veins with opposite side veins

The method described here, of borrowing pairs from the main rib and beginning the side vein, is one of several in current use, all of them equally successful. It is necessary to have at least seven pairs in the main rib in order to have one pair left behind, which is used to tie over the pairs returning from the side vein. If the main rib is made with fewer pairs, the extra pair/s needed must be hung in before making the edge stitch at 2 (fig. 47), and laid down inside the first downright thread. When the side veins are finished, the extra downright pair/s must be removed after the side vein pairs have been tied up between the bobbins of the downright pair of the main rib. Choose any threads out of the bunch, tie them three times and cut them off short.

If the main rib is made with more than seven pairs, work as described in the pattern and tie the returning side vein pairs between the bobbins of the nearest downright pair.

Raised vein with staggered side veins

The procedure described for opposite side veins is unsuitable where (as in the second leaf, fig. 51) a side vein diverges from the pinhole side of the main rib and there is no side vein directly opposite. The reason for this is that a dent would be made in the main rib where the single downright pair is tied over the returning pairs from the side vein. The method shown in fig. 52, i.e. including the runners in the side vein, gives an extra downright pair to preserve the smooth outline on the plain side of the main rib.

Note that the pinholes of the side veins are always made on the same side as the direction in which the main rib is being worked so that, after rolling back, the side vein pairs can more easily be incorporated into the main rib without having to be passed round a pin (fig. 77).

When making branching side veins, always work first the branch that is furthest from the direction in which the main rib is being made (fig. 78).

Sometimes it is more convenient to make a raised vein up the middle of a leaf instead of down, so that it finishes near the top of the leaf. In such a case, work the runners to the plain side after the last pin of the rib has been set, and tie them three times. Tie all the other pairs three times, cross the two outer pairs under the bunch, and tie them three times over the bunch. Bow off the bobbins but do not trim the ends. When this hole needs to be used for the clothwork of the leaf, raise the pin, lift up the bunch of thread ends and make the sewing under it, without removing the pin. The ends of thread can be trimmed short when the clothwork has been completed.

Joining half stitch (or whole stitch) clothwork to an underlying rib

Two methods were shown in this pattern. The first, *joining by means of a downright pair*, is only used when working in half stitch and when the underlying rib is running in the same direction as the rows of weaving, as in the half stitch flowers. The other method, *joining by means of the leading runner thread* (fig. 50), is the more common and is used where the rib being crossed lies at a different angle to the rows of weaving. This method should always be used when working in whole stitch, as it involves only one thread, its partner continuing the weaving in a straight line.

Adding new pairs along a sewing edge

The method described in the large leaf (fig. 56) is one of several. Another is to slide the new pair over the runners when they have arrived at the sewing edge and lay it to the back of the pillow. Then make the sewing. Before working back, bring down the new pair and lay it in position.

Another method is to add the new pair whilst making the sewing. This may be done either as shown in fig. 24, laying the pair across the loop before passing the second bobbin of the sewing pair through the loop, or by passing one of the bobbins of the new pair through the loop before completing the sewing. In both cases, tie the sewing pair once when the sewing has been completed.

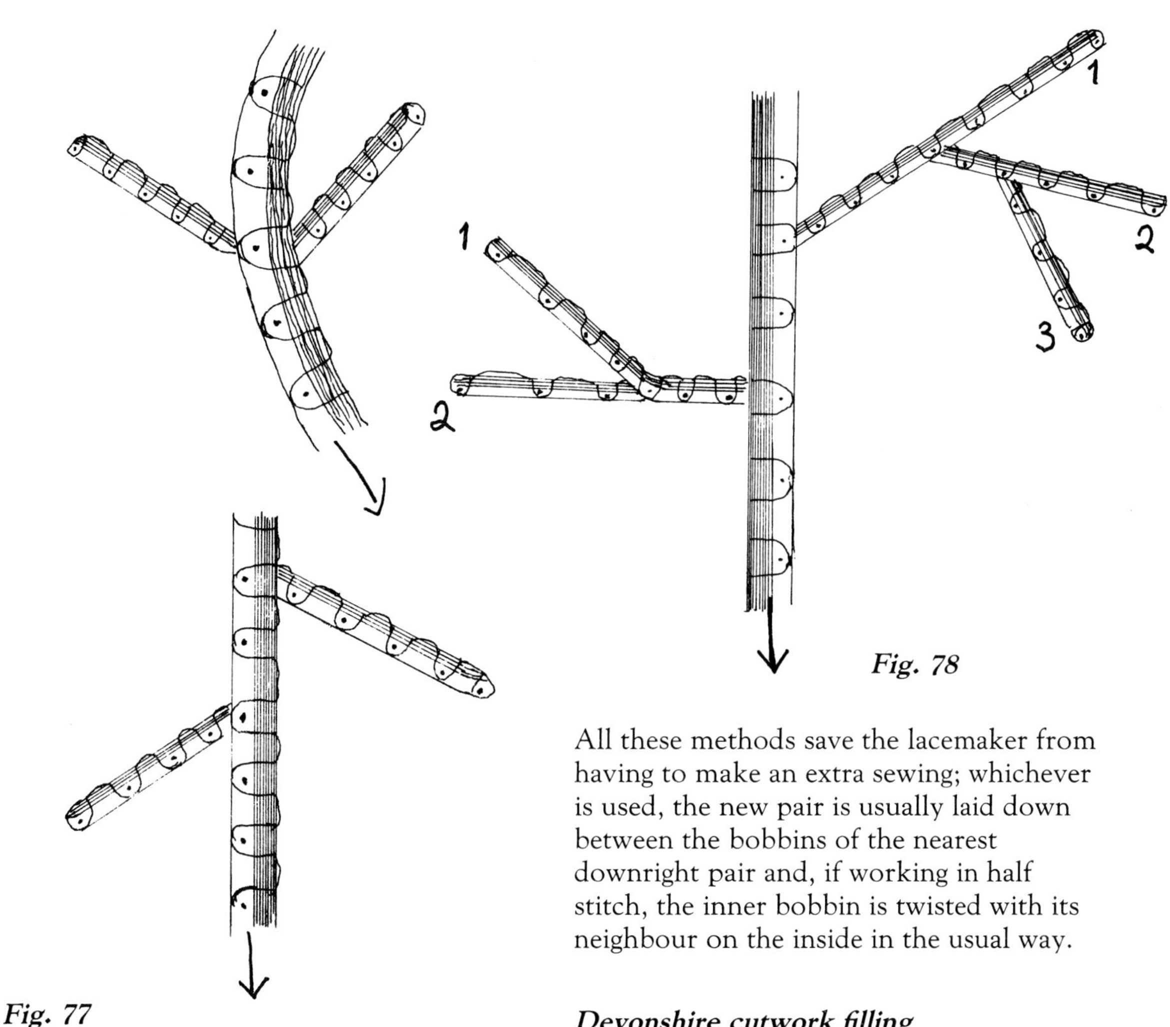

Fig. 78

Fig. 77

All these methods save the lacemaker from having to make an extra sewing; whichever is used, the new pair is usually laid down between the bobbins of the nearest downright pair and, if working in half stitch, the inner bobbin is twisted with its neighbour on the inside in the usual way.

Devonshire cutwork filling

This is one of a variety of fillings featuring swing leadworks, which occur often in Honiton lace. All are made without a pricking and in all of them it is important to weave all the leadworks in a row with the same weaver. This (and the twists between) prevents the last leadwork from pulling out of shape while the current one is in progress, and also makes it possible to pull the vertical pairs into place again without distorting the leadworks.

— 4 —
Cone Flower

Fig. 79 Cone Flower

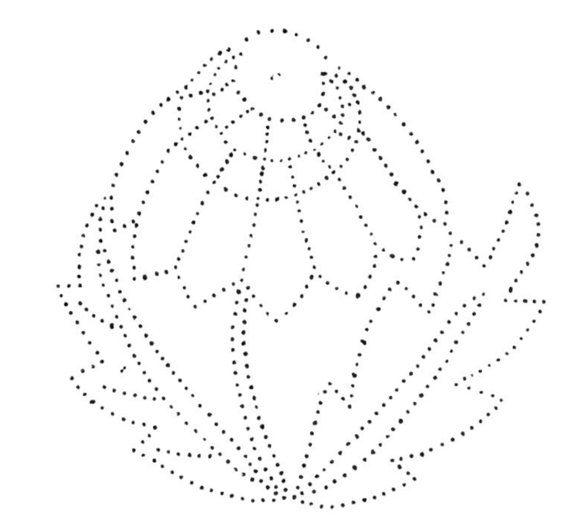

Fig. 80 Pricking for Cone Flower

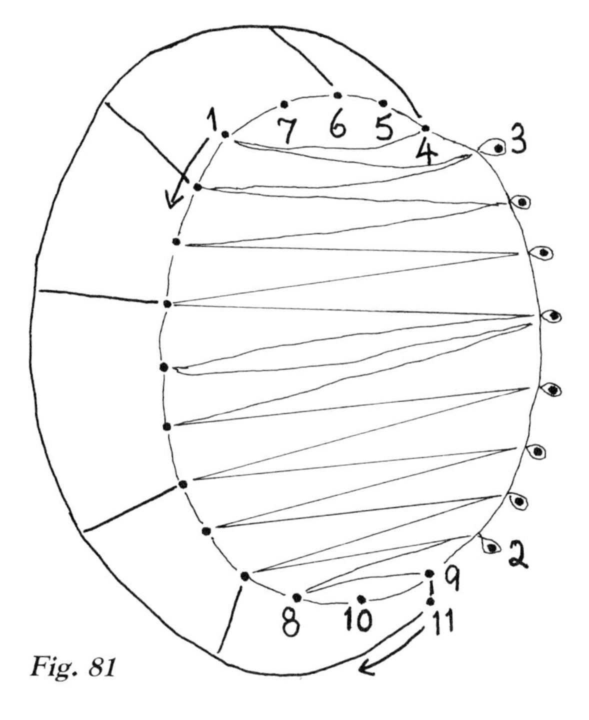

Fig. 81

Set up at 1 (fig. 81) with seven pairs and a magic thread, and rib anti-clockwise round the centre circle of the flower. From 2 to 3 inclusive make a purl edge, reverting to an ordinary edge at 4. Hang in and lay back two new pairs at this hole, and also at 5. At 6 and 7 hang in one new pair and also lay back a pair from the rib (making thirteen pairs altogether). Work to the plain side from 7. Sew the runners, and also the edge

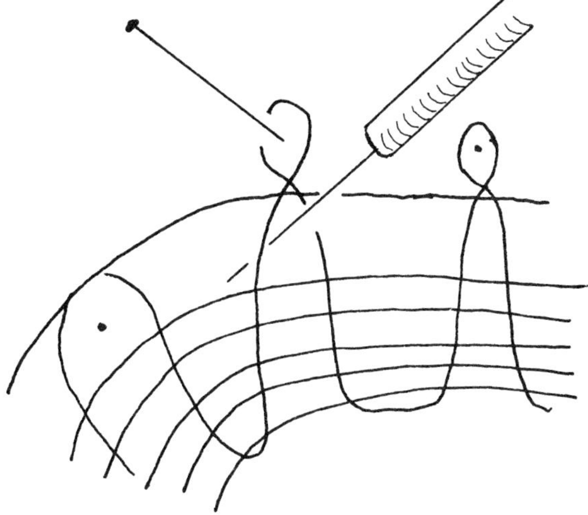

Fig. 82 Sewing inside a purl edge

pair on the other side, to 1. Tie both these pairs twice.

All the pairs are now used to fill in the circle with half stitch. Turn the pillow so that 1 is at the top. Straighten the threads, ensuring that the new pairs that were hung in and those that were laid back from the rib are in order and have not got caught up round any pins. The remaining pairs from the rib should lie to the left of these pairs, hanging down between 7 and 1. Take the outermost pair on the right (hanging from 4) as runners across all pairs in half stitch, but making a whole stitch with the first and last pairs. Leave the runners, tie the last pair they passed, and work back with it in half stitch, making a whole stitch with the last pair. Top-sew the runners at 3, hooking the runner thread round one of the side bars inside the twisted edge pair, as shown in fig. 82. Raise, but *do not remove the pin* for the sewing, otherwise the purl will be distorted. Continue to fill in the circle as shown in fig. 81, sewing twice into one of the purl-pin holes. Discard six pairs from both sides in the last few rows, leaving seven pairs at the end. After 8 work one more row in whole stitch through all but the last pair, sew the runners to 9, and tie them twice. Sew the unworked downright pair also to this hole, tie it twice and twist it three times to become an edge pair. Sew the two outer pairs of downrights on the left at 10, tying the outer pair twice.

This pair is now used as a runner pair for the rib that runs outside the centre ring and connects to it at intervals by means of side veins. To begin the rib, work the tied pair from 10 through all but the twisted pair on the outer side. Twist, set pin 11 and make the edge stitch with the twisted pair.

The side ribs are made with four pairs borrowed from the main rib, as described in the last pattern (*see* figs. 42 and 43), the only difference being that, when the last hole of the side rib has been made, the runners work back to the plain side and are sewn with an edge sewing to the centre ring. Tie the runners twice, place the other three pairs between them and tie them twice again over the bunch. Roll back and incorporate the pairs into the main rib as before.

Before the main rib joins to the centre ring, lay back a pair from the rib at 1 and 2 (fig. 83), then work to the plain side and top-sew

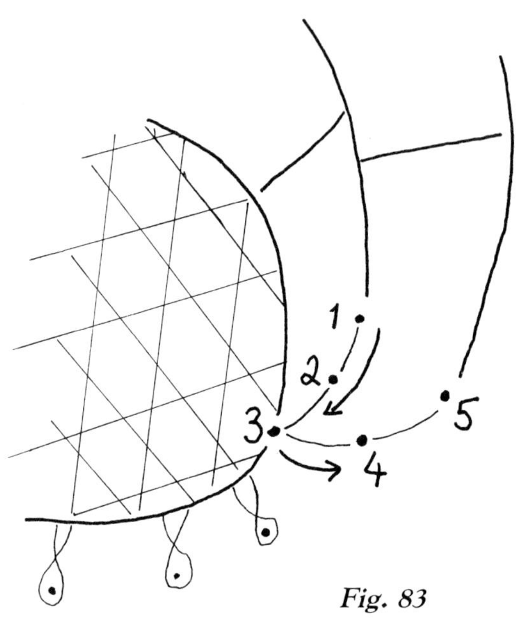

Fig. 83

the runners to the upper bar of 3. Make a whole stitch with the sewn pair and the nearest downright pair. Top-sew this downright pair to the lower bar of 3, tie it once and twist it three times. Turn the pillow in order to work the next section of rib. Untwist the edge pair at 2 and use it as runners to work through the downrights on its left towards 4. Twist, set the pin and make the edge stitch with the twisted pair from 3. *Take the pair laid back at 2, bring it out between pins 2 and 1, and lay it down to the right of the downrights. Work the runners from 4 through the downright pairs and through the added pair, and leave the runners to become passive. The added pair is the new runner pair and it works to 5 to make the next edge stitch. Repeat this procedure with the pair laid back at 1, working from * and bringing this pair out to join the downrights from between pin 1 and the preceding pin. Continue the rib and side ribs, joining to the inner rib.

The turn into the rib which goes up the side of the first petal is made in a similar way to the turn on the other side. Lay back a pair from the rib at 1, 2 and 3 (fig. 84), work to the plain side and sew the runners with an edge sewing to 4. Make a whole stitch with the runners and the nearest downright pair. Sew the downright pair to 5 with an edge sewing, tie it once and twist it three times (leaving the sewn runner pair to become downrights). Untwist the edge pair on the pinhole side, use it as a runner pair to work through the two downright pairs, and make hole 6, using the twisted pair from 5 to make the edge stitch. Work back through the downright pairs and also through the pair that was laid back at 3 (first bringing this pair out between pins 4 and 3 to lie next to the downrights). Leave the runners and use the added pair as new runners to work to 7. Repeat this process, bringing in each of the other two pairs that were laid

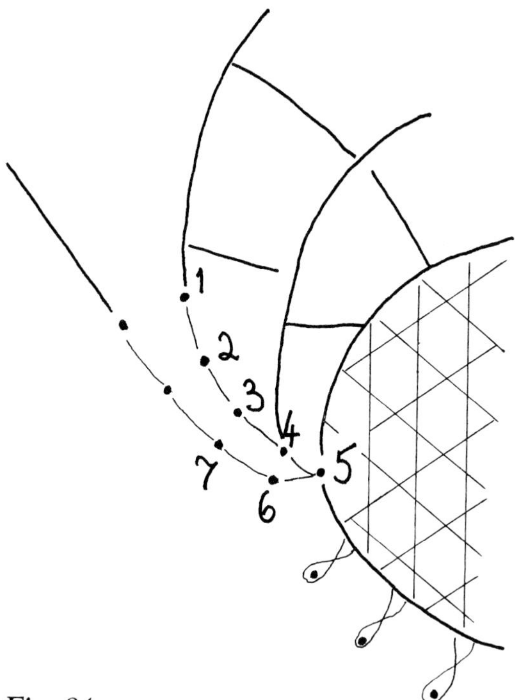

Fig. 84

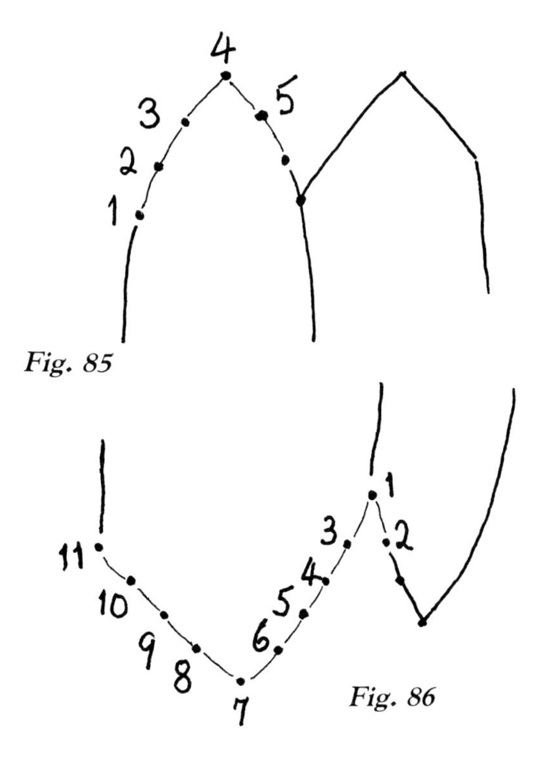

Fig. 85

Fig. 86

back to work the next two holes. Continue the rib, with normal turning stitches on the plain side, up the side of the petal.

Hang in and lay back a new pair at 1 (fig. 85). At 2 hang in and lay back a new pair, and also lay back a pair from the rib. Lay back a pair from the rib at 3. Rib to 4, turn the pillow and work back down the petal in whole stitch. Add another new pair at 5 (giving ten pairs altogether) and gradually bring in the pairs laid back on the rib side. A vein, made by twisting the runners, is made down the middle. After the last hole on the right, work to the outer side and top-sew the runners. Before returning, sew out the edge pair into the nearest hole of the outer semi-circular rib. Tie this pair twice and lay it back, but do not cut it off. Work the runners from the other side across, and top-sew them into the same hole. From now on the runners are top-sewn on both sides. Discard pairs as the petal narrows and sew out the last few pairs at the end. Bunch, and tie back the little bunch, using a couple of the discarded pairs. Cut off all but the pair that was laid aside.

Sew two new pairs into the same hole in which the edge pair was sewn out, laying these beside this pair. Sew three new pairs into the next hole of the semi-circular rib. These six pairs make a rib up the side of the completed petal. Use the outer pair on the left as runners, work them through the other pairs and sew them to the last hole made before the edge pair was sewn out. Continue the rib, making turning stitches on the left. On the right sew into each hole of the petal – these may be either edge sewings or raised sewings (edge sewings were used in the sample).

After the sewing at 1 (fig. 86), work to the plain side and, before returning, sew in a new pair at 2 as an edge pair. Continue the rib, hanging in and laying back a new pair at 3, 4, 5 and 6. Also lay back a pair from the rib at 5 and 6. Rib to 7 and turn. Work down the petal as normal, gradually bringing in the pairs that were laid back and hanging in new pairs at 8, 9 and 10 (giving fourteen pairs altogether). Remember to tie the runners at 11. When all the laid-back pairs have been used, top sewings are made on the left into the holes of the previous petal, ignoring the rib, which is left as a raised ridge on the other side of the work, as if it were a roll.

Gradually discard four pairs – two from each side – in the last few rows. It will also be necessary to back-stitch once or twice near the bottom of the petal to slope the weaving slightly, so that from a sewing at 1 (the last hole in the side of the previous petal, *see* fig. 87) the runners can work to 2, where they begin a back stitch. (Alternatively, if there is already a back stitch waiting to be made up at this hole, use it once more, i.e. twist the runners once, remove the pin, replace it in the same hole under the runners, and work back without making up the edge stitch.) Work back through all pairs and top-sew the runners to the right bar of 3 (the hole that was used to sew in the new rib pairs).

**Work the runners through one pair, tie them once, then work them through two more pairs and leave them. *With the last pair the runners passed through, work back through two pairs to the left and top-sew this pair to one of the bars of 4. Counting from the left, and not including the

Fig. 87

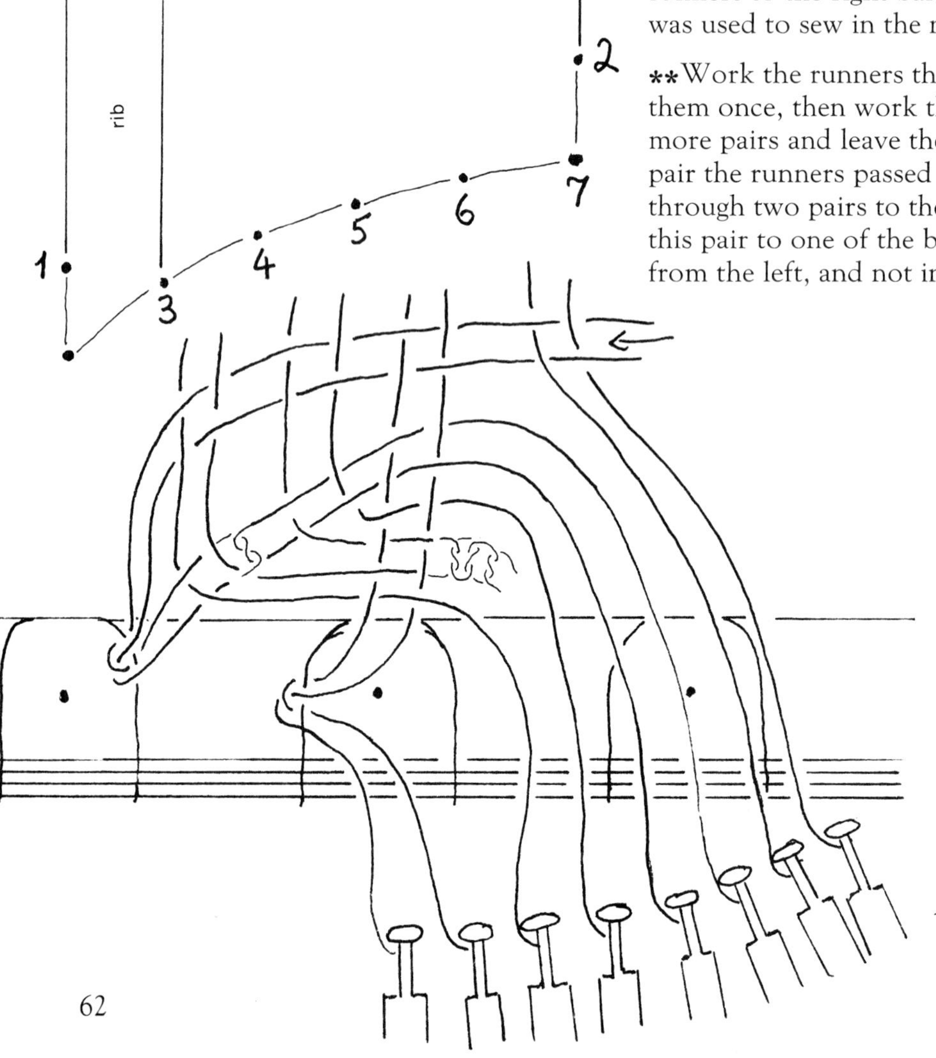

Fig. 88

runners, take the second and third downright bobbins, tie them three times and lay them back (fig. 88). Work the sewn runner pair through three pairs to the right, then leave it. Repeat from * for holes 5 and 6. When the pair has been removed after the sewing at 6, work the runners through all remaining downright pairs and make up the back stitch at 2. Work back and sew the runners at 7. Tie the second and third downright threads and lay them back. Tie the sewn runners twice, lay the remaining five pairs between these bobbins, and tie them twice again over the bunch. These six pairs will rib up the side of the petal as previously, after all the discarded pairs have been bowed off, the ends trimmed short and the pins tidied.

The next petal is worked similarly, nine more pairs being hung in around the top (two pairs at one hole on the pinhole side after the pillow has been turned), making a total of sixteen pairs. Reduce to twelve pairs before the end of the petal has been reached. Arrange the rows so that, from a back stitch begun in the last hole on the pinhole side, the runners are worked through and sewn to the right bar of 7. This hole corresponds to hole 3 in the previous petal. Continue as described, working from **.

If more than the required number of bobbins (six pairs in this case) remain after the last sewing along the base line before the bobbins are bunched, the surplus pair/s may be removed on the pinhole side both before and after making up the back stitch.

Use sixteen pairs for each of the next two petals, and fourteen pairs for the following one. Do not cut off all the discarded pairs at the end of this petal; leave one, or even two, on the right-hand side at or close to the last pinhole, to fill in a gap in the last petal at this point.

The last petal is made with ten pairs and is worked straight down, making top sewings first into the side of the previous petal, then into the outer semi-circular rib. After the first sewing into this rib (made into the same hole from which the rib along the side of the petal originates), remember to tie the runners when they have passed back through the first downright pair. Discard pairs in the next few rows and sew out the remaining few, bunching and tying back the bunch, using two of the discarded pairs.

The leaves have an open mid-rib with leadworks, which is made first. Set up at the tip of the mid-rib of the full leaf at 1 (fig. 89) with ten pairs hung 'open' round the pin, i.e. making sure that the bobbins of a pair do not lie next to each other. Twist all pairs twice and insert a magic thread. Make a whole stitch with the two outside pairs on the right, twist both three times and work the inner of these pairs through all but the last pair on the other side. Twist the runners three times, set pin 2 under them

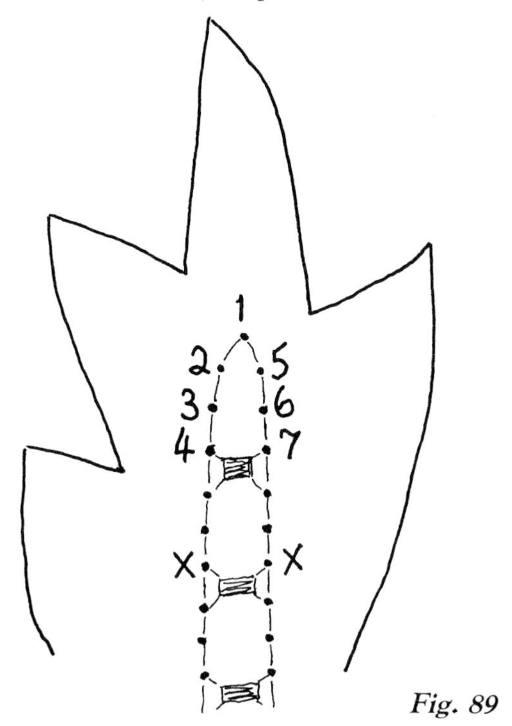

Fig. 89

and make the edge stitch with the last pair. Split the bobbins into two groups with five pairs in each. Make a whole stitch using the innermost pair from each group, and leave. Whole-stitch the runners from 2 through three pairs to the right, including the nearest pair from the middle whole stitch. Make a turning stitch with this pair and work back to 3, where the next edge stitch is made. Work one more row of rib with these five pairs, leaving the group after the edge stitch at 4.

The remaining pair from the middle whole stitch is the runner pair for the right-hand rib – work it through three pairs to the right and make the edge stitch at 5 with the last pair. Rib two more rows with this group, working holes 6 and 7. *Work the runner pairs from 4 and 7 to the middle, twist them once and make a shallow leadwork with them, not quite touching the sides of the ribs. If the leadwork is made too wide (or deep), it will look untidy when the ribs are continued. Twist both pairs once. Leave the pair that contains the weaver, tucking the tail of the weaver bobbin under one of the cover cloths to keep the thread slack. With the other pair work back to the outer edge on its own side, working three more holes of rib and stopping after the edge stitch at X. Now return to the other leadwork pair and use it as runners again, working three more holes of rib as far as X on the other side. Repeat from *, making a leadwork after every three holes of rib.

Work as far as the edge stitches at 1 and 2 (fig. 90) at the bottom of the leaf. Discard one downright pair from each rib. Work the runner pair from 2 back through one downright pair and leave it to become passive. Take the innermost downright pair from each side, make a whole stitch with them to join the two ribs, and leave. Work the runner pair from 1 through all except

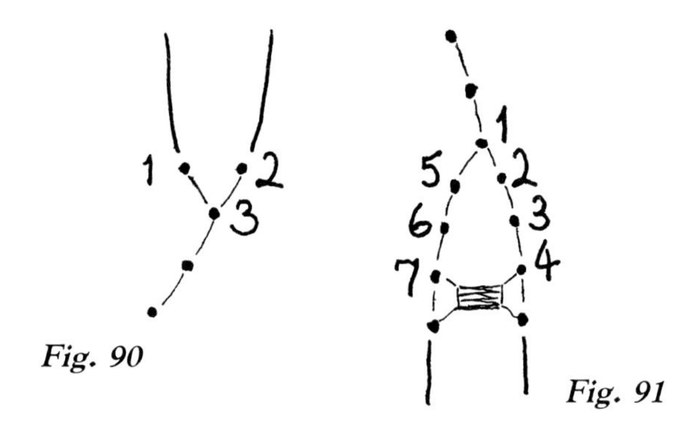

Fig. 90

Fig. 91

the edge pair on the other side, and make hole 3 with this. Continue the rib with these eight pairs, making turning stitches on the left and pinholes on the right, to work the little stem that connects the two leaves. Work to the point where the next open vein begins.

When the edge stitch has been made at 1 (fig. 91), give three twists to the outermost pair on the left. Divide the threads into two groups of four pairs. Take the innermost pair from each side and make a whole stitch with them. Whole-stitch the runners from 1 to the middle, including the nearest pair from the central whole stitch. Make a turning stitch with this pair and work back to 2, where a new pair is hung in before the edge stitch is made. Work two more rows of rib on this side, hanging in a new pair at 3 and 4, and leaving the runners at 4. Return to the left-hand rib, using the remaining pair from the central whole stitch as runners and working them through two pairs to the left. Twist them three times, set pin 5 under them, hang in a new pair and make the edge stitch with the twisted outside pair. Continue the rib, hanging in a new pair at 6 and 7 (seven pairs in each rib) and again making leadworks after every three holes.

The side veins on the right side are made at the same time, as described in the last pattern (fig. 52). When the pairs have been rolled back, it is a little tricky to tie them back into the main rib, as they enter from a different angle and the weight of the bobbins tends to pull the knots open. When you have laid the side vein pairs between the bobbins of the first downright pair of the main rib, pick up the bobbins of this pair and hold them in the right hand. With the left hand pick up the four side vein pairs and place them to the back left of the pillow (having first pressed down the pins of the left-hand rib). The downright pair can now be tied firmly twice over the bunch, and the bunched pairs brought forward and laid into place.

In the few rows following the last leadwork, discard two pairs from each rib. The joining of the two ribs is as already described, except that the pinholes of the following single rib are made on the left side. Therefore, after throwing back a further pair from each rib, working the *left* runners back through one pair and joining the two ribs with a whole stitch made with the two inner pairs, work the *right* runners through to the left to make the next pinhole there. Continue the rib, laying back a pair at each subsequent hole until five pairs are left, and at the last two holes joining to the adjacent flower petal (*see* Glossary, *Sewing to Join Two Edges*).

After the pin and join at the top hole, turn the pillow and fill in the point of the leaf with half stitch, bringing in the last of the pairs which were laid back from the rib (cut off the rest). These six pairs will be sufficient for the first two or three rows. Then add a new pair on the pinhole side. On the other side, top-sew into the single rib and then into the nearest of the two ribs of the open vein when this is reached. It will be necessary to sew twice into one or two of the rib holes, so that from a sewing to the upper bar of 1 (fig. 92) the runners can work to 2. After setting the pin here, hang in two new pairs before making the

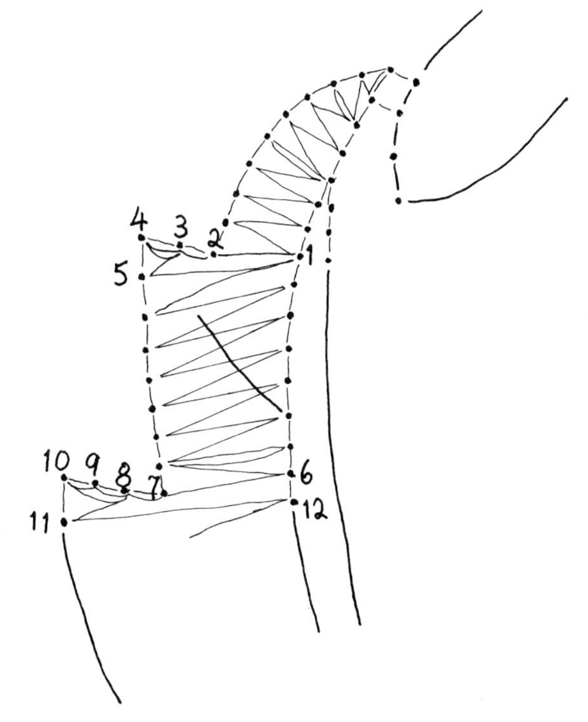

Fig. 92

edge stitch. Do not twist these pairs as one normally would for half stitch – just lay them down side by side between the bobbins of the first downright (whole stitch) pair. Make the edge stitch.

Change to whole stitch to work the serration. ∗Work the runners back through two pairs and leave them. Take the last pair the runners passed, work it through one pair to the left, twist it three times∗ and set pin 3 under it. Hang in two more pairs and make the edge stitch. Repeat ∗ to ∗, set pin 4 and make the edge stitch. Work back through one pair, tie the runners, then work them through one more pair, and leave them. Tie the pair the runners have just passed through once, work it through one pair to the left, and make the edge hole at 5.

Change to half stitch again, working the runners through all pairs and top-sewing them to the lower bar of 1. Continue in half stitch, joining the leading runner thread to the top hole of the side vein when reached (fig. 50, p. 38), and again half-way down the side vein. Reduce to eight pairs just before the next serration is reached, and arrange the rows so that, from a sewing to the upper bar of 6, the runners will work to 7, where two new pairs are hung in before the edge stitch is made. Change to whole stitch and work along the line to the point as described above, hanging in two new pairs at 8 and two more at 9. Work to 10, make the edge stitch and tie the runners when they have returned through the first downright pair. Work in half stitch through the next two pairs, and in whole stitch through one more pair. Leave the runners and tie the last pair they passed through. Work with this pair in half stitch through the next two pairs to the left, and in whole stitch through the last downright pair. Make the edge stitch at 11. Work back through all pairs to the other side. Gradually reduce to eight pairs again before the next serration.

This serration is made similarly to the previous one as far as the point, two pairs being hung in at each hole except the last (giving fourteen pairs altogether). However, the line of holes here lies at the same angle as the weaving – it does not slope back like the previous serrations. Therefore, after making the edge stitch at the outermost hole, change to half stitch and work back through all pairs (remembering to tie the runners at the point) to the next sewing on the other side. Complete the half leaf, reducing to seven pairs near the end – these will be used to make the stem to the flower.

When the sewing has been made to the upper bar of 1 (fig. 93), tie the runner pair twice and leave it. Top-sew the nearest

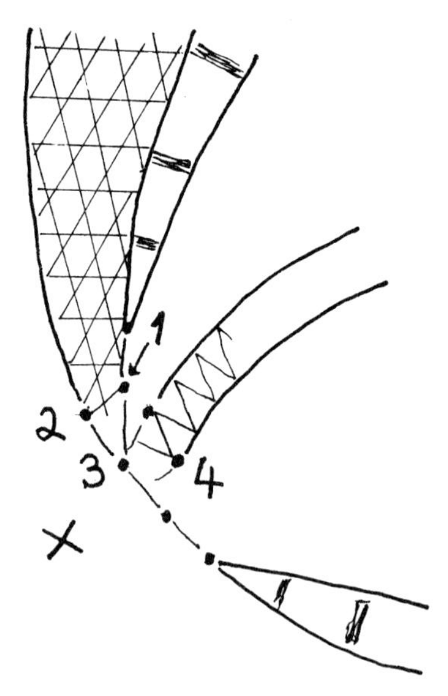

Fig. 93

downright pair to the same bar and use it as runners to work to 2, making a whole stitch with the first and last pair, in the usual way. Work back in whole stitch, sew the runners to the lower bar of 1, and tie them twice. Lift both the sewn and tied pairs over the rib, to lie over the stem to the flower. Lay the next two downright pairs beside them. The last two downright pairs are top-sewn to the upper bar of 3, and the edge pair is sewn to the lower bar of 3 and tied twice. Replace pin 3 and lift these sewn pairs over the rib, to lie beside the other pairs. Bow off the discarded pairs, trim the ends and tidy the pins. Turn the pillow to work the stem.

Tie two coarse threads to a pin and set this at approximately X. Lay these bobbins in position as fifth from the right and third from the left. Give three twists to the outside pair on each side. Use the second pair from the right (one of the tied pairs) as runners, work it through the nearest coarse pair, tie it once, then work it on to 4. Tie the runners again here, when the edge stitch has been made and the coarse pair worked. Continue the stem, gradually reducing until

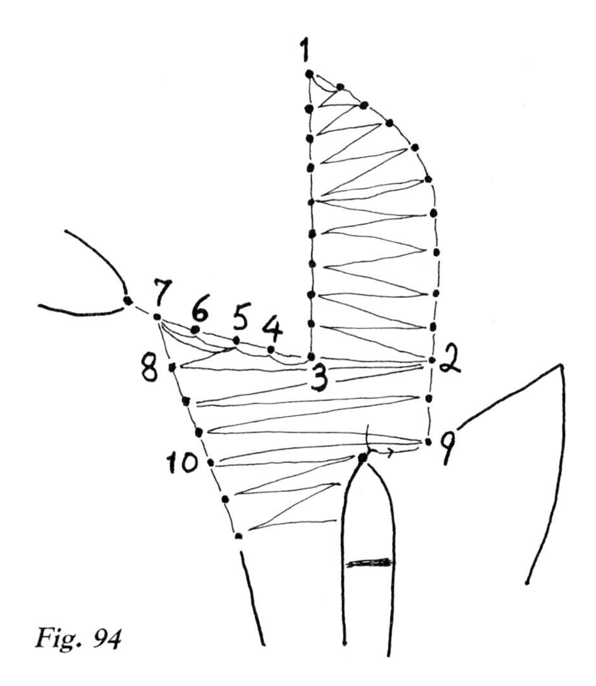

Fig. 94

only five pairs remain for the last few rows. Sew out into the flower.

Begin the other leaf by setting up with six pairs and a coarse pair at 1 (fig. 94), and adding pairs on the right side only until there are twelve pairs in all. One back stitch will be needed on the left before the first serration is reached. Begin a back stitch at 2 and work to 3, where two new pairs are hung in before the edge stitch is made. Work from hole to hole of the serration as before, hanging in two new pairs at 4 and 6. At 5 hang in two new pairs, placing these inside the coarse thread as usual, and also one new pair, which is slid up the runners and laid to the back of the pillow before making the edge stitch (fig. 95). At 7 join to the topmost hole of the adjacent flower petal. Work back through the coarse pair,

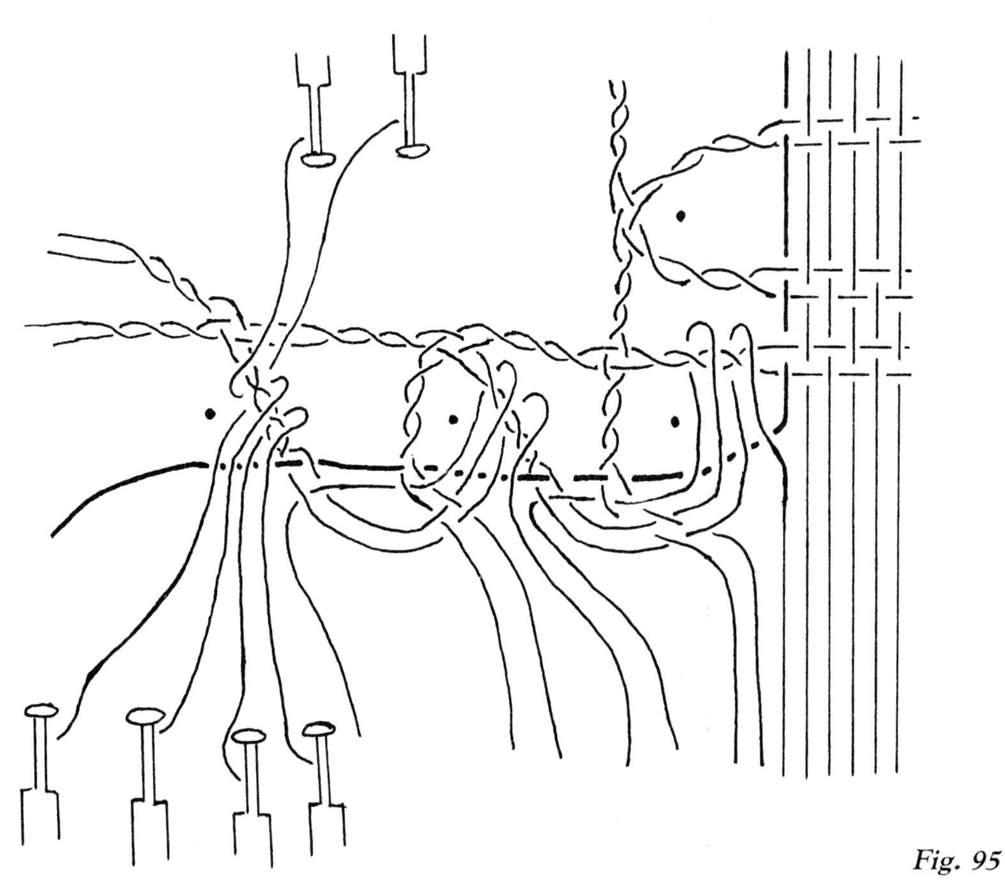
Fig. 95

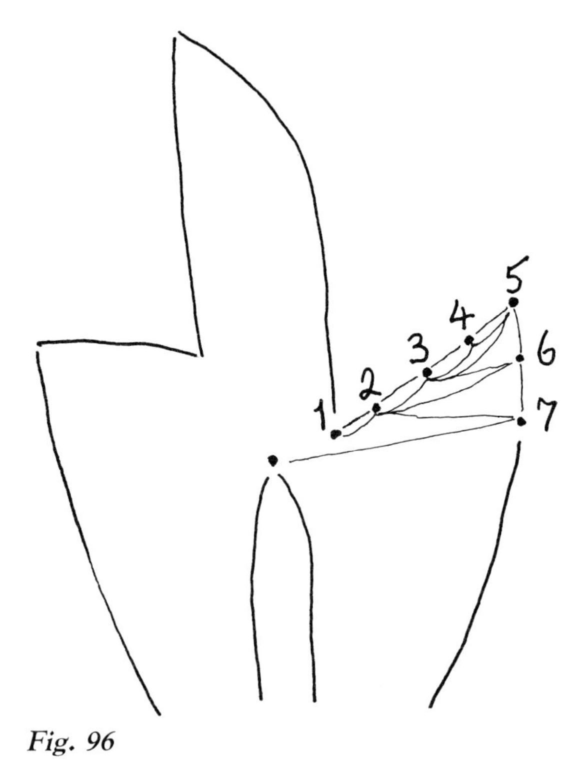

Fig. 96

tie the runners, then work them through three more pairs. Leave the runners, tie the last pair they passed through, and work back with this pair to 8. Take the pair from the back of the pillow and lay it into the gap to the right of the old runners and of the single thread hanging from 5. Work the runners from 8 through all downright pairs and make up the back stitch at 2.

Continue the clothwork, discarding two pairs on the left before 9 is reached. Begin a back stitch at 9, work to 10 and leave. The work now divides. Not counting the edge pair, take the fifth downright pair from the right and sew it to the topmost hole of the vein, using the magic thread. This will be the runner pair for the right side; work it through the next pair on its right, tie it once, then work it through the remaining three downright pairs to 9, where it makes up the back stitch. Hang in two new pairs at the same time, and leave.

Return to the runners left at 10, work them to the middle, sew them also to the top hole of the vein, then continue working the left side of the leaf, reducing the number of pairs as it narrows before the next serration. Here again two new pairs are hung in at each hole except the last, together with one extra pair, to be laid to the back at the hole corresponding with 4. When the last hole at the point has been worked, bring the runners back through six pairs, leave them, tie the last pair they passed through and work it back to the outer edge. Before returning, bring down the pair from the back of the pillow and lay it into the gap. Make the last serration in the same way and finish the section, sewing out the last few pairs into the centre vein and tying back the little bunch. Bow off, but do not trim the ends until the other half of the leaf is made.

This second half was left with two new pairs hung in and the edge stitch made at 1 (fig. 96). Work back and forth as usual along the line of the serration, hanging in two new pairs at every hole except 5, and also hanging in and laying back a pair at 2 and 3. This line slopes back a little more than the points in the first half of the leaf, and consequently two holes have to be worked along the outer edge before the runners can weave across to the vein side. After the edge stitch at 5, work back through four downright pairs (remembering to tie the runners at 5), *leave the runners, tie the last pair they passed through and work with it to 6. Bring down the pair that was laid back at 3 to lie to the left of the old runners and to the left of the single thread hanging from 3. From 6 work back through seven downright pairs and repeat from *, working to 7 and bringing down the pair laid back at 2, before working back through all pairs and sewing the runners to the top vein hole. The next point is made in the same way.

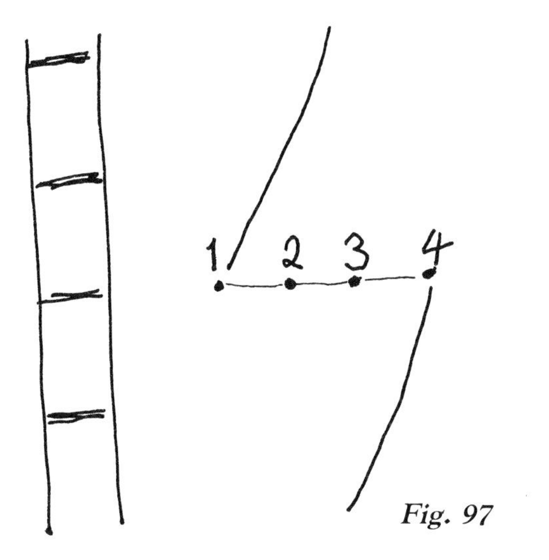

Fig. 97

The last serration on this side is almost level with the direction of weaving, and here a variation of the method can be used. Before making the edge stitch at 1 (fig. 97), *hang in one new pair, laying it down inside the coarse thread as usual. Slide another new pair up the runners and lay it to the back. Make the edge stitch. Work back through two pairs, leave the runners, take the last pair they passed through and work with it through the coarse pair, twisting it three times and setting a pin under it into the next hole along the horizontal line. Repeat from * until the pin has been set at 4. Do not hang in a new pair here – just make the edge stitch. Bring down the pairs that were laid back, and lay them into the spaces made where the downright pairs were pulled out of position when they were taken as runners at each hole. Work from 4 through the coarse pair, tie the runners, then work through all pairs to the vein side. Complete the section, reducing the number of pairs and sewing out into the vein at the end. Tie and bunch. It is not necessary to tie back the bunch here, as the ends will be hidden by the finished part of the leaf.

Working Methods

Before embarking on a Honiton pattern, study it carefully to work out the order in which the various sections are to be made. Often there are two or three ways of carrying out a design, all of which would look equally good. In such a case choose the course requiring as little sewing-out and restarting as possible, since each finishing, however well made, is a potential weak point in the fabric. Both this pattern and the last show some ways in which threads can be carried on from one part of the pattern to the next, but no book can describe what to do in every situation. Every design presents its own problems, and how these are solved depends largely on each lacemaker's skill and ingenuity.

In the petals of this flower ribs have replaced the more commonly used rolls. A. Penderel Moody, writing in 1907 (*Devon Pillow Lace: Its History and How to Make It*, Cassell & Co. Ltd), noted that 'The rolled raised work is classed as plain work, and though often used in very fine work, it cannot compete with ten-stick or gimp [ribbed].' She thought that 'the reason why some workers are inclined to look down upon [rolled work] is that it is sometimes made loosely, while the stem stitch [rib] does not lend itself to careless treatment.' She had a point – looking at some old Honiton lace, though admittedly not the best, one can see that the little rolls have not always survived very well. Given the adverse economic conditions suffered by Devon lacemakers during much of the nineteenth century, it is hardly surprising that they cut corners and tried to save time wherever they could. The winding pair was twisted two or three times round the bunched threads, and the roll was attached to the braid only once or twice along a long run. It might not be attached at all if there were just a short distance to the top of the next tap, so that in some examples the roll lies loosely on top of the lace and can easily be pushed out of place. Penderel Moody herself suggested that the roll should be attached at every third hole of the braid, but even this does not give a very satisfactory result. Today, when speed is no longer of such vital importance where lacemaking is concerned, time can be spent making the rolls firmly and neatly. The lacemaker can choose either method, and there is very little difference in appearance unless a magnifying glass is used – if anything, a rib is slightly wider than a roll made with the same number of pairs, and it does not take much longer to work than a carefully made roll.

Ribbed vein with leadworks

This is normally made with ten pairs, as in the whole stitch leaf. In the half stitch leaf extra pairs were added to the ribs in order to avoid having to hang in, and afterwards take out, additional pairs each time a side vein was made. Also, as the opposite rib formed the outside of the leaf, the two extra pairs provided a more substantial edge.

When designing a pattern with raised side veins joining to an open vein with leadworks, as here, try to arrange the side veins in such a way that they will join the open vein in between leadworks and so avoid complications.

Decreasing along a horizontal base line

This procedure is used at the base of the flower petals. As so often in Honiton lace, a basic technique has to be learned and then adapted to suit the shape being worked. The points to remember in this method are that a back stitch should be started at the last hole on the side furthest from where the decreasing begins; the runners should be tied after the first sewing on the base line (or after the first pinhole on the base line, if a pinhole edge is being worked along this line at the same time, as in the next pattern); and the threads that are tied and discarded are the second and third downright threads nearest the runners.

If a finer thread is being used, or if the holes along the base line are more widely spaced, it would be necessary to sew twice into each, thus discarding two pairs per hole instead of only one.

If the base line slopes a little, as in fig. 98, it might be advisable half-way along to work through all downrights to use the back stitch pin once more (in order to fill up the extra space), before completing the base line and finally making up the back stitch.

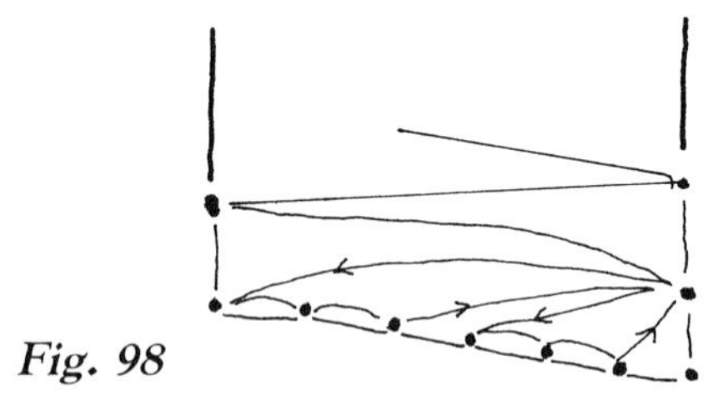

Fig. 98

Increasing along a horizontal or backward sloping line

The serrations on the leaves show that here again there are adaptations of a basic technique, and which of these is used depends on the size of thread in relation to the spacing of the pinholes, on the position of the holes in relation to each other, and on the shape being worked.

Check that the last pinhole to be used on the straight side before beginning to work along the extending line (hole 1 in fig. 99) is level with, or slightly above, the first hole of the extending line (hole 2), never below it.

If a pinhole edge is being made on the straight side, it is also necessary to decide in advance where the runners will go when the point has been completed – whether they will travel to 5 or, if this leaves too much of a gap between the rows, whether hole 1 needs to be used again. If so, a back stitch will have to be started *before* the extending line is begun. (An example of this technique occurred in the whole stitch leaf, where a back stitch was started at 2 in fig. 94 so that this hole could be used again after the completion of the point.)

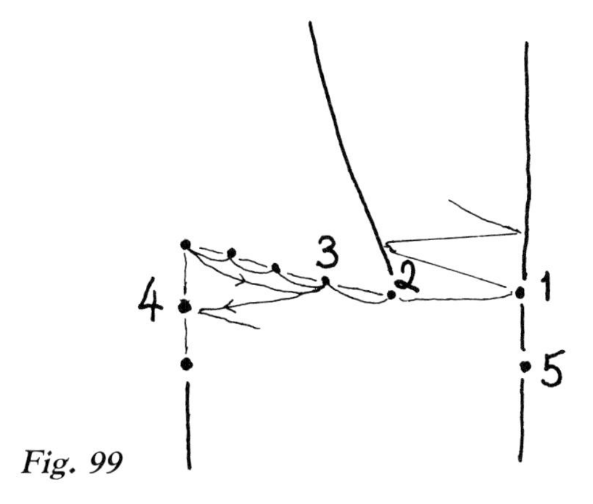

Fig. 99

The number of new pairs to be hung in at each hole along the extending line is also subject to some variation. When working in half stitch, two new pairs per hole are usually sufficient, and some workers hang in only one new pair per hole. In this case one still works back through two pairs after making the edge stitch and before abandoning the runners.

The third pair that is laid to the back of the pillow is sometimes useful where one or more rows must be worked to fill in the little points, as is mostly the case in this pattern. Here one has to plan the course of the runners beforehand, to determine where to hang in the third pair. For example, in fig. 99 hole 4 has to be worked before the runners can go across to the straight side. So after making the outermost pinhole of the point, the runners need to work back to a hole slightly above the level of 4. Hole 3 is in approximately the right position, and this is the hole at which to hang in and lay back a third pair, to cover any gap made by the downright pair being pulled out of position as new runners.

Some lacemakers automatically hang in and lay back a third pair at every hole of the extending line, so that they are there if needed – any that are not can easily be removed without waste of thread by bowing off close to the knot that connects the pair. When the holes along the extending line are closer together, or if a thicker thread is being used, or if the line slopes steeply backwards, the third pair is not usually necessary.

—5—

Treble Clef

Fig. 100 Treble Clef

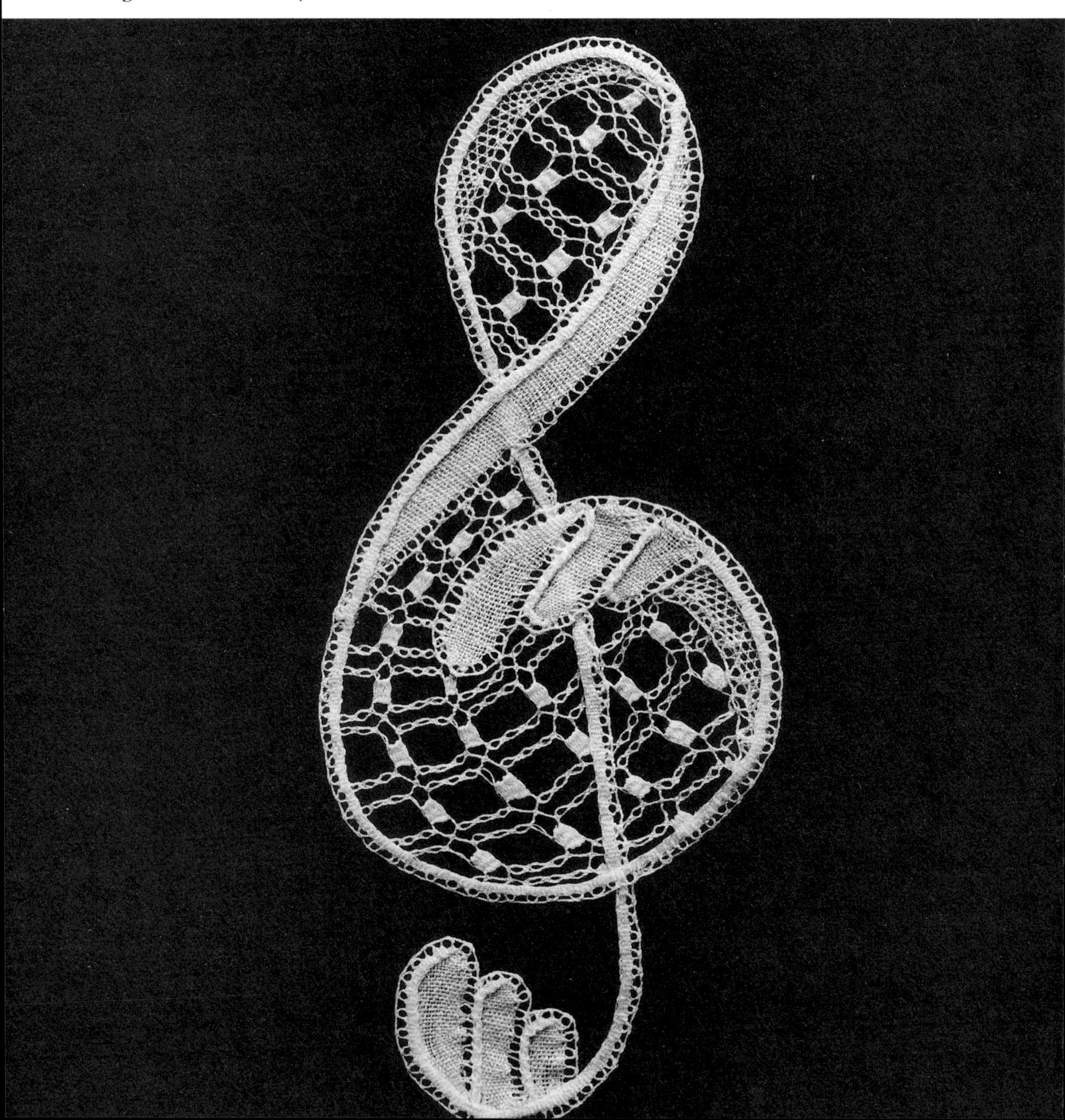

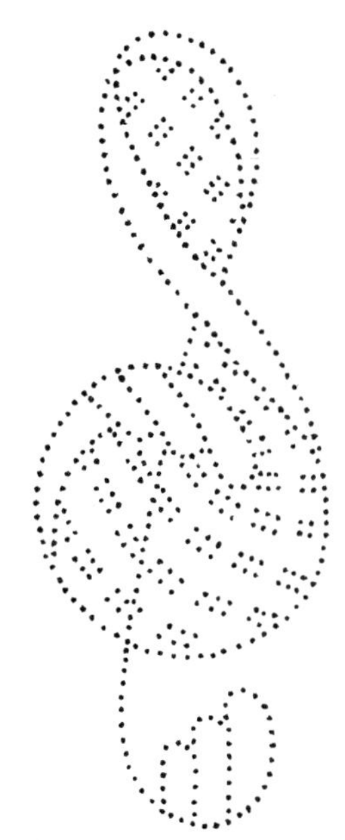

Fig. 101 *Pricking for Treble Clef*

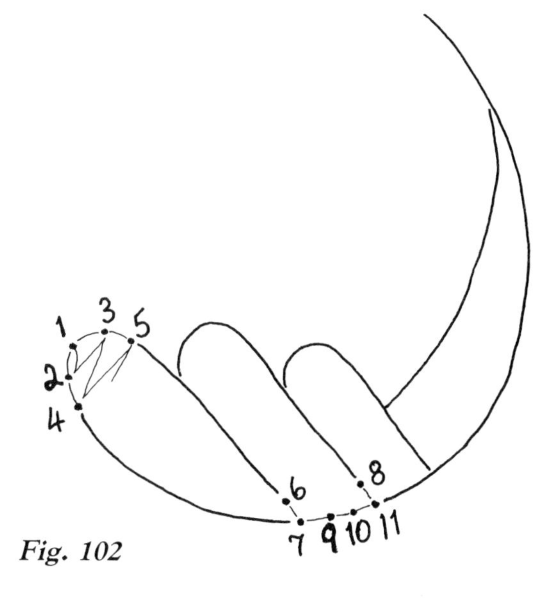

Fig. 102

Begin with the taps at the centre of the clef, setting up at 1 (fig. 102) with eight pairs and a magic thread (no coarse pair), and work like a flat Honiton leaf, adding a new pair at 2, 3, 4 and 5. Near the end of the leaf reduce to eight pairs and arrange the weaving so that from 6 the runners will work to 7. After the edge stitch at 6, lay aside but do not cut off the second and third downright threads on the right side. Work to 7 and make the edge stitch.

Taps with a simultaneous foot edge

*Lay aside the left edge pair. Open the runners, lay the remaining five pairs between these two bobbins and tie them firmly twice over the bunch (fig. 103). The tied pair is now used as a winding pair to make a roll up the side of the last tap. Use the pair laid aside at the end of the last tap to attach the roll. The edge pair that was laid aside at 7 should be pushed well out of the way and perhaps covered with a cover cloth – it will not be needed again until the end of the next tap. This tap is made as usual, using the roll pairs to rib across the top and hanging in three more pairs to make ten pairs altogether (not counting the edge pair that was laid aside). Do not discard any pairs as you near the end of the tap.

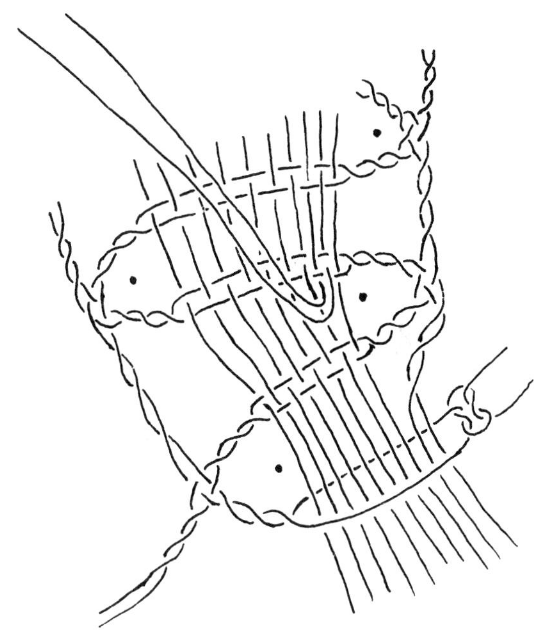

Fig. 103

Arrange the rows so that from a back stitch begun at **8, the runners can work across to be sewn to the right bar of 7 (fig. 102). This may sound awkward, but it is in fact an easy sewing to do – the pin can be removed and the little side bar is quite distinct, as the formation of the roll from here tends to keep this hole open. Replace the pin, work the sewn runners back through one pair, tie them once, then work them through two more pairs and leave them. Take the last pair they passed through as new runners back through two pairs to the left, twist them three times and set pin 9 under them. Take up the edge pair that was laid aside at 7 and use it to make the edge stitch at 9. Take the second and third downright threads, tie them three times and lay them back. Work the runners through three pairs to the right, leave them and work back with the last pair they passed through to 10**. When the edge stitch has been made here, and the second and third downright threads tied and laid back, discard another downright pair from the other side, leaving eight pairs altogether, then work through to 8, to make up the back stitch there. Lay aside (but do not cut off) the second and third downright threads counting from the right, and work from 8 through the remaining four downright pairs to 11, where the next edge stitch is made. Repeat from * for the beginning of the next tap, which will require two additional pairs hung in across the top.

Work back down this last tap, hanging in and laying aside two new pairs per hole at 1, 2 and 3 (fig. 104), as shown in fig. 105. These will be used later for the adjoining section of half stitch. Begin a back stitch at 4, which corresponds with 8 in fig. 102. Work the base of the tap, repeating ** to ** above. When the edge stitch has been made at 5 (corresponding with 10 in fig. 102), and the second and third

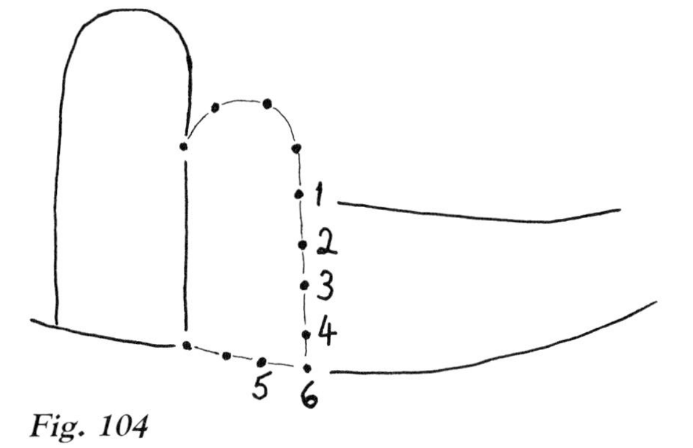

Fig. 104

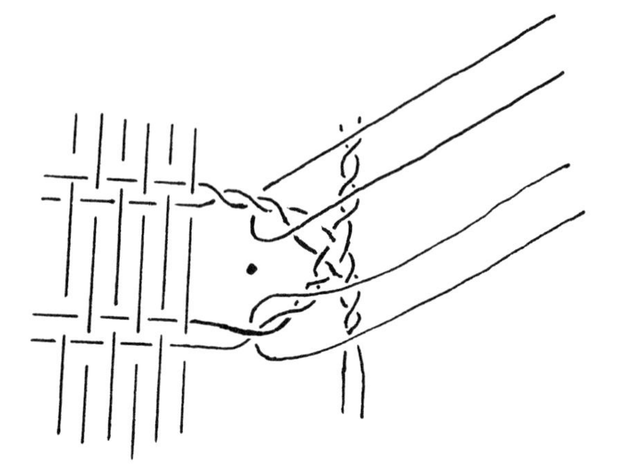

Fig. 105

downright threads have been tied and discarded, take the second and third downright threads from the right and lay them out to join the six pairs laid aside on this side. Then work from 5 to 4, to make up the back stitch, hanging in and laying aside one more new pair when the edge stitch has been made. Work to 6, then continue along the outline in rib with the seven pairs remaining (first taking the three twists out of the right edge pair, so that it becomes a downright pair). While working the outline, push the eight pairs laid aside for the half stitch section well out of the way. Work the rib, following the direction of the arrows in fig. 106, then leave these bobbins at about X.

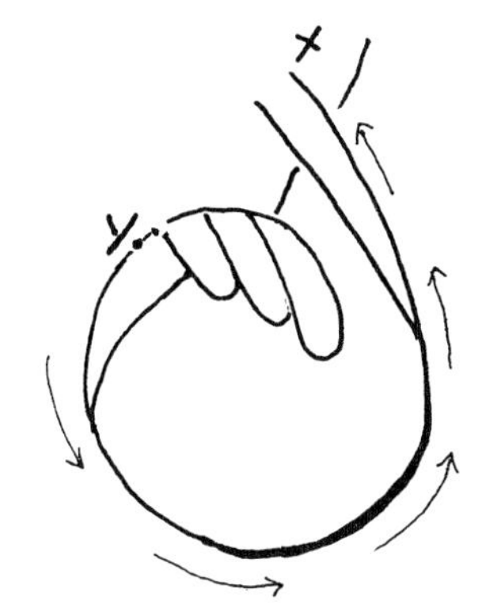

Fig. 106

Return to the bobbins that are waiting to do the half stitch section and lay them straight, ensuring that none of the threads have accidentally become entangled round pins. Give three twists to the outer pair on the right, and use the next pair as runners to work in whole stitch through the remainder and be top-sewn to Y. Change to half stitch and work this section, gradually reducing and sewing out the last few pairs into the rib. Bunch, and tie back the little bunch, using two of the discarded pairs on the rib side. Bow off, but do not trim the ends until the filling has been completed.

Return to the rib and work to 1 (fig. 107). It may be necessary to make one or two back stitches before this point is reached in order to make the rib lie flat, as the pinholes here have to be made on the wrong side of a slight curve. It is advisable to distinguish hole 1 with a different-coloured pin (a yellow brass one if you are using white brass, or vice versa), or to put a scratch or mark on the pricking here. Having made the edge stitch at 1, change the side on which the pinholes are made and continue the rib along the outer line of the loop, hanging in and laying back one new pair at 2, 3, 4 and 5, two new pairs at 6, and one at 7. Work two or three more pins of rib, then leave these bobbins and turn the pillow.

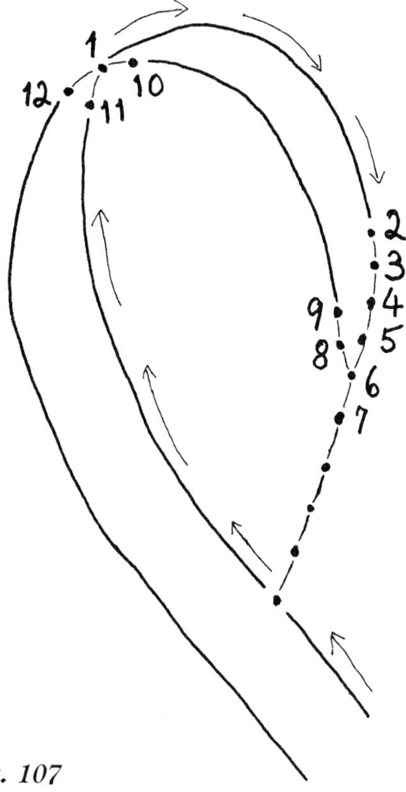

Fig. 107

Give three twists to the pair hanging from 7 and also to the right-hand pair of the two pairs from 6. Set pin 8 (almost hidden under the rib) under this pair, and make an edge stitch with the pair from 7. Work back in whole stitch through two pairs, leave the runners, tie the last pair they passed through and work back with it through one pair to 9, making the edge stitch. Work the runners to the left again, making a whole stitch with the first pair, a half stitch with the next and a whole stitch with the pair after that (hanging from 4). Leave the runners, tie the pair from 4 and work with it back to the pinhole side in half stitch, making a whole stitch with the last downright pair. Continue in this way until all the hung-in pairs have been brought in, then make top sewings on the rib side. Reduce to four or five pairs where the section narrows, and arrange the rows so that from 10 (the last hole on the pinhole side) the runners can work through to be sewn to the upper bar of 1. Twist this pair three times and leave it. Sew the edge pair from 10 to the upper bar of 11, then use it as a runner pair to work through to 12, making the edge stitch with the twisted pair from 1. This section is now worked in whole stitch, hanging in pairs in the normal way on the left until there are approximately thirteen pairs altogether, and making top sewings on the right. Reduce the number of pairs near the end and sew out the last few into the rib, tying back the little bunch of threads as before. Again, bow off, but do not trim the ends until the filling has been made.

Return to the rib pairs that were left hanging, and complete the last few holes to the whole stitch section. If preferred, the pairs can be sewn out here and new pairs sewn in on the other side. In the sample, however, the pairs were worked across to the other side: after the last rib hole, work the runners to the plain side, sew them to 1 (fig. 108) and tie them twice. Sew the edge pair on the other side to 2, and tie it twice. Work one of the sewn pairs through all the pairs to the other side, twist it once, pull up and leave it. *Work the last pair through which it passed to the other side through all pairs, twist it once and leave it (fig. 109). Repeat from *, pulling up carefully after each row until the plait has reached the other side of the whole stitch section. Sew the outermost pair on both sides to 3 and 4, and tie both pairs twice. Give two or three twists to the pair at 3 and, using the pair from 4 as runners, work the short length of rib, pinholes on the left. After the last hole work the runners through to the plain side. Here again, the pairs may either be sewn out into the tap leaf or worked across, as above. If using the latter method, sew one of the runner pairs to an underlying hole between the first and second taps when the

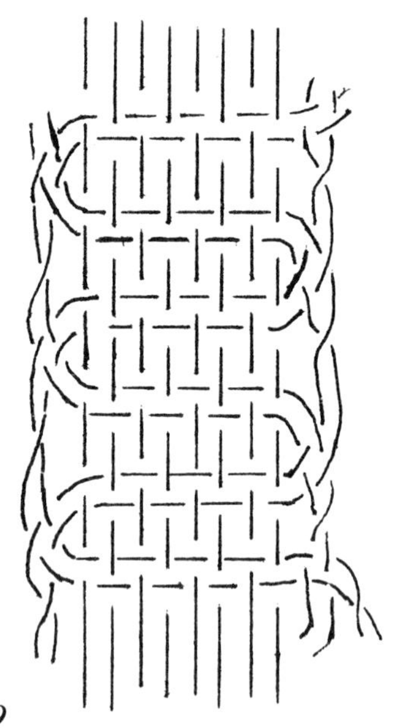

Fig. 109

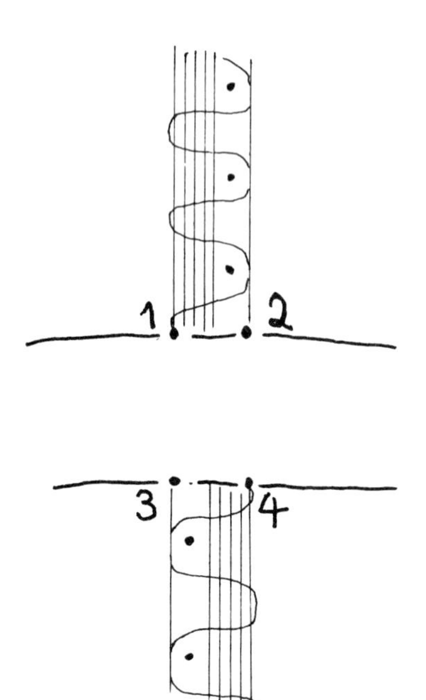

Fig. 108

plait has reached this point, so that not too much of a length of plait is left lying loosely on the wrong side of the lace.

Continue the rib on the other side of the taps, pinholes on the left, crossing over the rib that surrounds the filling (top-sewing the edge pair on one side and the runners at the plain side at the crossing.) Work right round the tail of the clef and up the side of the largest of the three taps that finish this curve. Hang in and lay back five new pairs across the top, making twelve pairs altogether, and make this tap and the following roll as described in 'Rosette' (pattern 2). The middle tap is made with ten pairs and worked across the base, as were the flower petals in the last pattern. A slight variation on the same method is used for working the base of the last tap, which also takes ten pairs.

Make the edge stitch at 1 (fig. 110); as this hole lies hidden under the rib, simply stick the pin through the rib into the hole. Work across, sew the runners at 2, tie them three times and lay them back. Top-sew the edge pair from 1 to the left bar of 3. Work this sewn pair back through one pair, tie it once, then work it through two more pairs and leave it. *Work the last pair through which it passed back through two pairs, and top-sew it to the right bar of 3. Take the second and third downright threads, tie them three times and lay them back. Work the sewn pair through three pairs to the right and leave it. Repeat from * using pins 4 and 5 twice, i.e. sewing first round the left, then round the right bar of each hole and removing one pair after each sewing. After the second sewing at 5, work the sewn pair through the remaining three pairs and sew it to 6. Leave the pair next to the sewn pair. Top-sew the other two pairs to 7 – one round each bar. Tie all four pairs three times. Replace pin 7, bringing the four tied pairs to lie between 6 and 7, and leaving the outline of the rib clear. Bunch and tie as usual. If preferred, the bunch can be tied back, using the two pairs discarded at 5, but this is not really necessary as the ends of the bunch will be well enough hidden by the outline rib and middle tap.

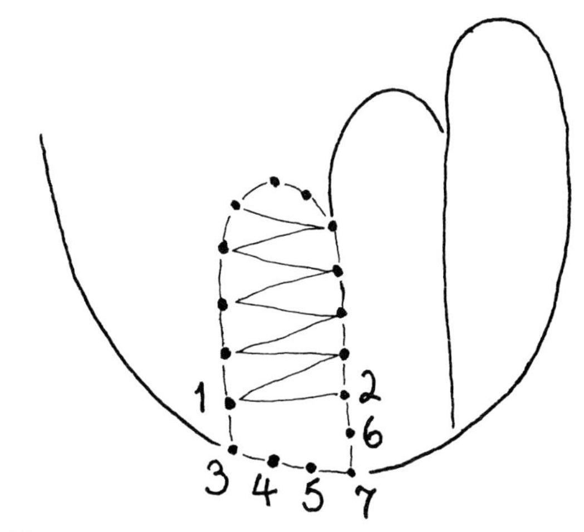

Fig. 110

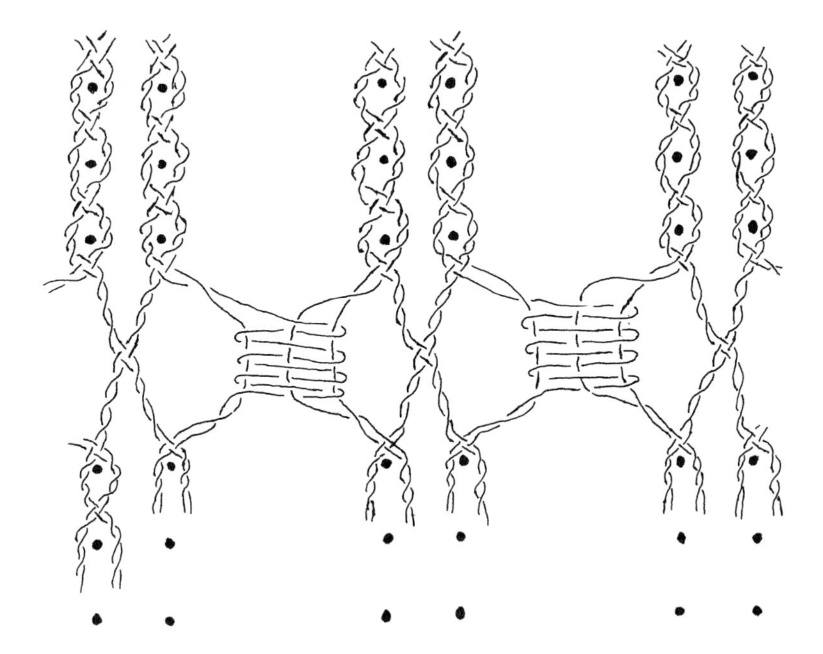

Fig. 111 *Six-pin chain and leadwork filling*

Six-pin chain and leadwork filling

This filling is illustrated in fig. 111. Four pairs are needed for each block of holes – two to work each of the two vertical columns – with a whole stitch and three twists, pin, as shown. When all six holes of a block have been worked and the lowest pins enclosed with a whole stitch, twist the two inner pairs of the block three times and cross them with a whole stitch and three twists. The outer pair on each side is twisted once and makes a leadwork with the outer pair of a neighbouring block (choose a bobbin without a knot in its thread to be the weaver). After the leadwork twist both pairs once. Each of these pairs now meets the nearest of the crossed pairs to work the next vertical column of three holes. Leave the leadwork weaver in the pair that will not be used next. Guard against making the leadwork too wide. The filling is best worked in horizontal rows, with all the six-pin blocks in a row, followed by the crossed pairs and leadworks, etc.

Sew in the pairs along the half stitch section of the upper loop of the clef, as shown in fig. 112, and make the filling following this diagram. Note that, in the second row of leadworks, the last one on the left requires only a few weaves across before the pairs are sewn out. This situation often arises with fillings that contain leadworks, when it is uncertain whether there is enough space at the side or end of the filling for a leadwork, or whether the pairs should just be sewn in at the edge. The golden rule is to make the leadwork when in doubt, even if it is only a fragment.

The start of the filling in the central space of the clef is shown in fig. 113. It is best to sew in the bobbins and complete the filling only as far as is shown in the diagram, then sew out the pairs at the holes marked X. Tie and bow off these fourteen pairs, but do not trim the ends. Remove the pins from this completed part of the filling. Now sew in all the pairs needed for the remainder of the filling and continue working in rows. Use

Fig. 112

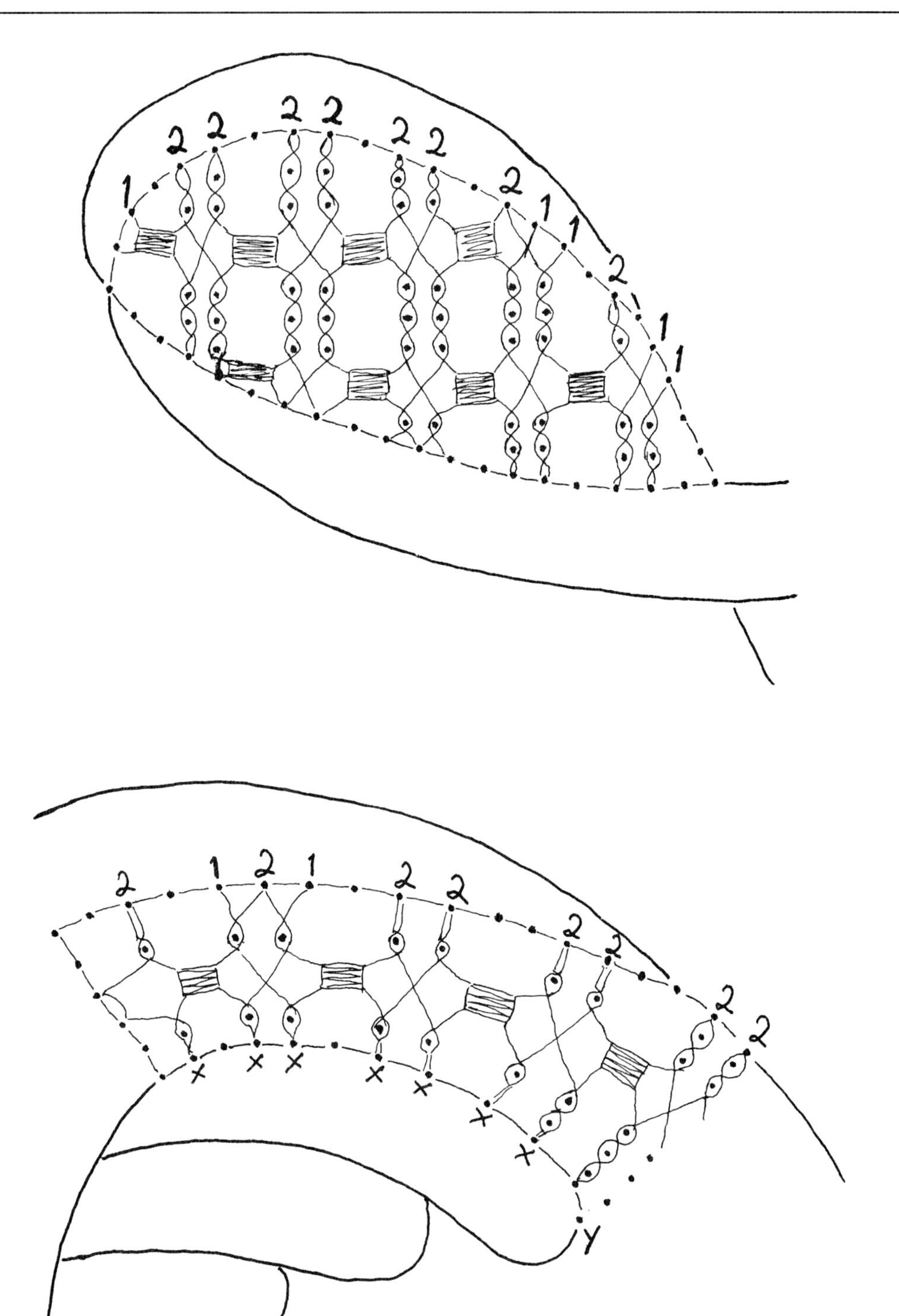

Fig. 113

the magic thread for the pair sewn out at Y or, failing a magic thread, make this sewing without removing the pin. When passing over the rib that crosses this space, make a top sewing using whichever pair is closest to the pinhole. This does not have to be done with every pair that crosses over the rib – two or three sewings will be sufficient over the whole space to fasten the filling and rib together here and there. Where a hole in the rib coincides with a hole in the filling and a sewing is not wanted, simply use the hole again, i.e. make a whole stitch and three twists, set the pin in the appropriate rib hole, and cover the pin with the next stitch.

Workings Methods

Taps with an integral base edge

In this pattern the edge pair for the base line was already present for the start of the second tap and only needed leaving behind when the roll was being made. However, if a raised edge is needed for the first tap, as in fig. 114, begin at A, hanging round the pin the number of pairs required for the rib, plus one extra pair and a magic thread. Make the rib to the top of the tap (leaving the extra pair hanging at A) and work back. From a back stitch begun at B, work to A and use the magic thread or, failing this, sew the runners without removing the pin. From now on the work proceeds as described for this pattern, with the hanging pair, twisted three times, used as the edge pair for the next hole along the base line.

When making the pricking for a pattern that uses this method, ensure that hole B in fig. 114 is quite close to the base line, so that the clothwork at the end of the tap is neat and dense, and has a firm edge.

Reversing braid, raised on one side

This occurs in the top loop of the clef and is also a useful method when working some types of leaf with a reversing tip, such as the one shown in fig. 115. Here the ribs are on opposite sides from those in the clef, but the procedure is similar. In each case the pinhole side of the rib is changed at the junction of the two sections and, when the top section has been filled in, the runners work through from the last hole on the

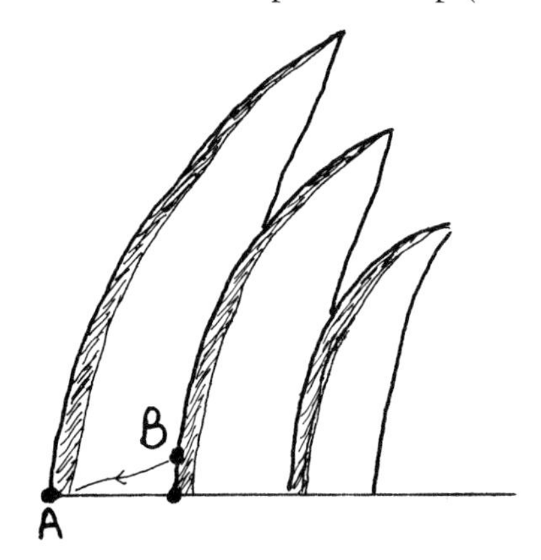

Fig. 114

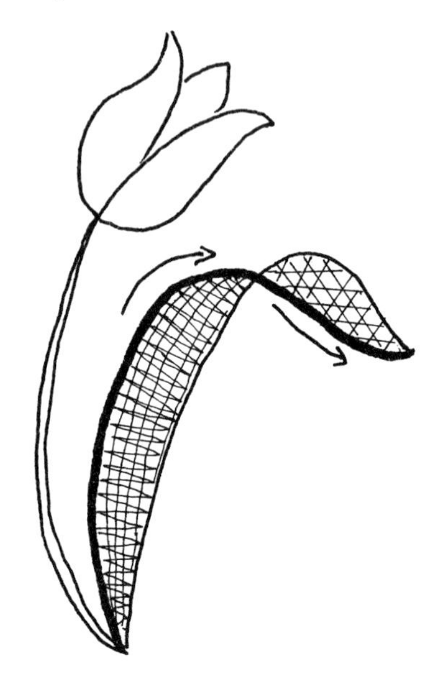

Fig. 115

pinhole side to be sewn to this hole and left to become the edge pair for the next section. The former edge pair is sewn to the next hole of the rib and becomes the new runner pair.

Shaped fillings

In recent years fillings have mostly been plotted on graph paper and worked straight, but this has not always been the case, and in some older Honiton laces one can occasionally see fillings which have been made to follow the curving outlines of the spaces in which they are set. There is scope for experiment here – the most successful fillings seem to be the ones that have clear lines crossing each other at right angles, for instance Blossom and Diamond. However, not every filling lends itself to this treatment (and none of those that are worked without a pricking), nor is every space to be filled suitable. However, where appropriate, this method of accommodating a filling to a curving space can add movement or flow to a design.

It is best to plot such a filling on a photocopy, drawing or tracing of the pattern (not on the pricking), using a well-sharpened pencil and with an eraser handy. A grid has to be drawn to fit into the space and a description follows of how it was done in this pattern, but it is only a suggested method – there may be easier or more convenient ways.

First decide which way you want the filling to curve, then draw in one of the main directional lines of the filling. In fig. 116 this represents the usually horizontal line of leadworks. This filling is normally plotted over a 1 mm grid, as shown in fig. 117, and it can be seen that there is a distance of 5 mm from the centre of one of the horizontal rows of leadworks to the centre of the next. Draw in the next and all subsequent leadwork rows 5 mm apart, following the line of the first row (fig. 118).

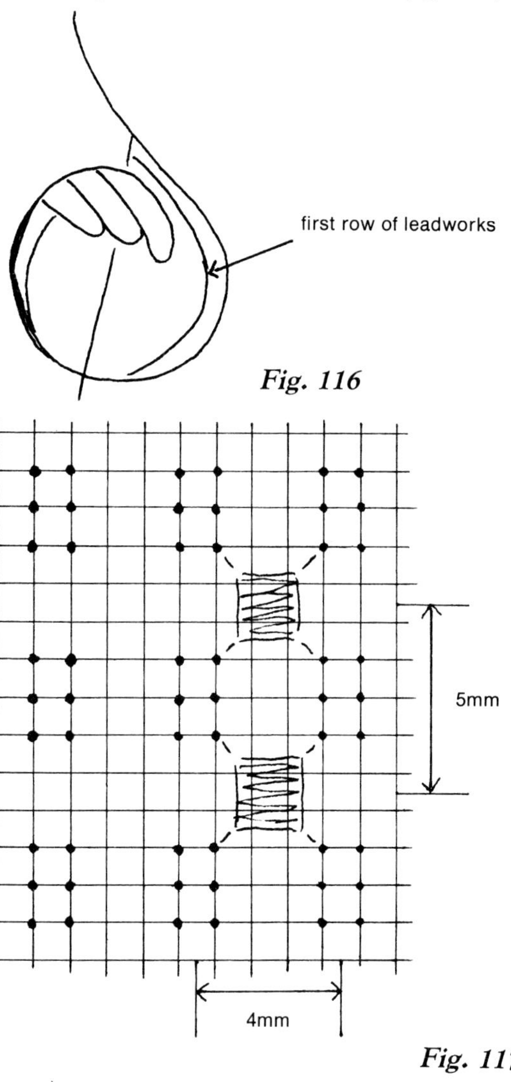

Fig. 116

Fig. 117

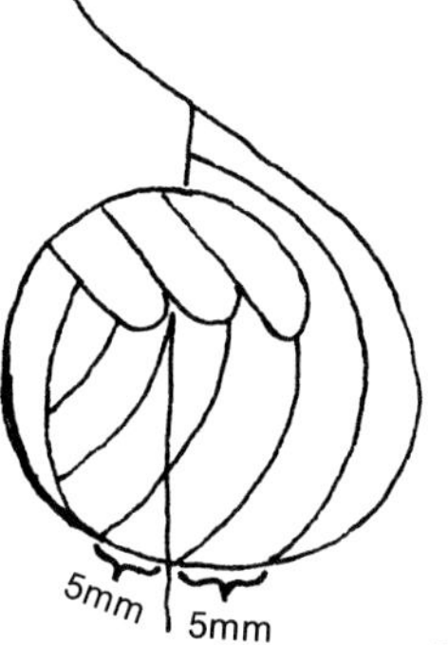

Fig. 118

This has to be done free-hand, but it helps to prepare a template from a slip of paper with two marks 5 mm apart on one edge. Position the template so that one of the marks coincides with the first drawn line. Slide it down this line, making dots above the other mark as you do so (fig. 119), then join up the dots.

Now draw in the first line for the vertical rows of the filling (fig. 120). It can be seen from fig. 117 that there is a 4 mm gap between the centre of one six-pin block and the centre of the next; these lines are therefore drawn approximately 4 mm apart. They have also been made to change direction gradually, so that in the narrow space at the top they still cross the leadwork line at approximately a right angle – otherwise the filling would become too distorted (fig. 121). The pinholes can now be plotted on both sides of these lines, 1 mm apart in both directions.

Fig. 120

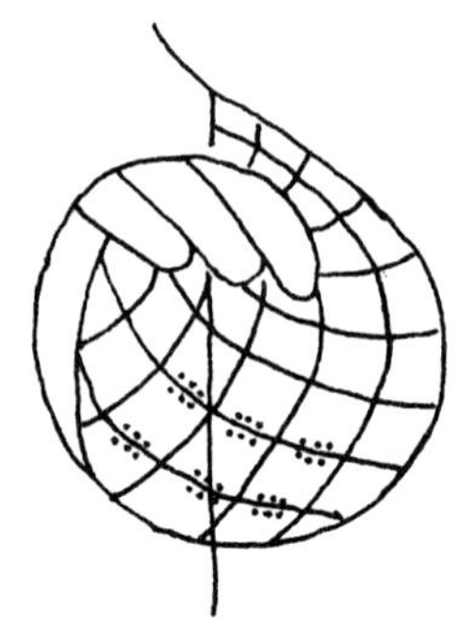

Fig. 121

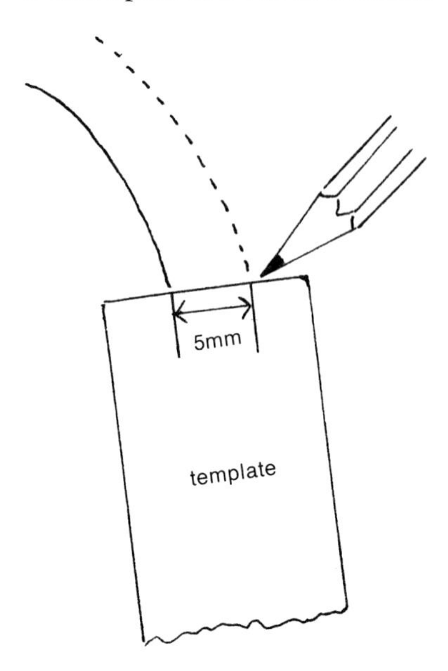

Fig. 119

Fig. 122 (right) *Umbellifer*

— 6 —

Umbellifer

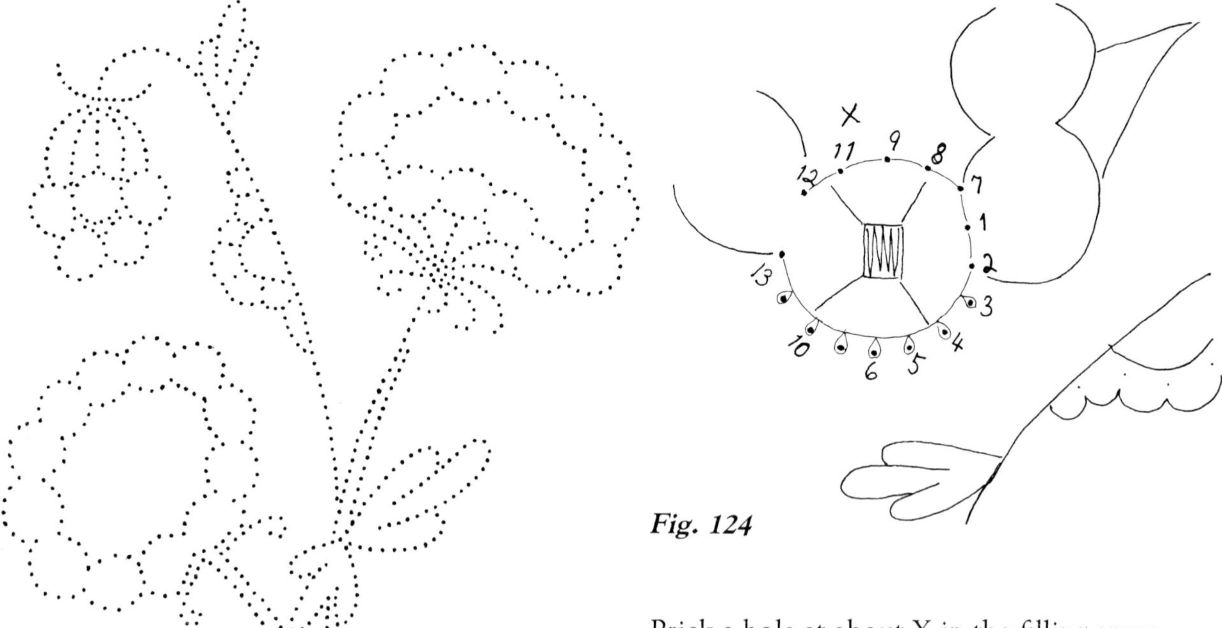

Fig. 124

Fig. 123 *Pricking for Umbellifer*

Begin with the flower to the right of the caterpillar and set the pillow so that the pattern faces you, as shown in fig. 124. This beginning is a little unconventional but it makes the sewing-out more satisfactory. Take fourteen pairs and lay one bobbin from each pair in front of you, letting the other bobbin dangle over the back of the pillow. Take all the bobbins hanging over the back of the pillow in one hand, twist the threads once round a large glass-headed pin or hat-pin, and push this in down to its head at the back of the pillow. Gently pull the bobbins in front of you until their partners have come to rest against the pin.

Prick a hole at about X in the filling space and set a support pin here under the outermost left pair of the seven pairs in front of you, so that this pair lies to the left of the pin. Using this pair as runners, work through five pairs to the right, twist three times, set pin 1 and make the edge stitch with the last pair (fig. 125). Work in rib to pin 2. In this flower and in the other large flower it is advisable to use the turning stitch described in the Glossary (p. 11, *Turning Stitch, b*). Continue the rib, but making purls along the outer edge, beginning at 3. After making the purl at 5, work back to the plain side through all but the last pair (this is now left out for the leadwork). Make the turning stitch, work back and leave after making the purl at 6 and the subsequent stitch and three twists.

Turn the pillow. Remove the pin holding the other set of bobbins and lay these straight. Give three twists to the pair on the outside of pin 1. Remove the pin at X and use the pair that was supported by this pin as runners to begin the rib on this side of the ring, working holes 7 and 8. After 8, work to the plain side through all but the

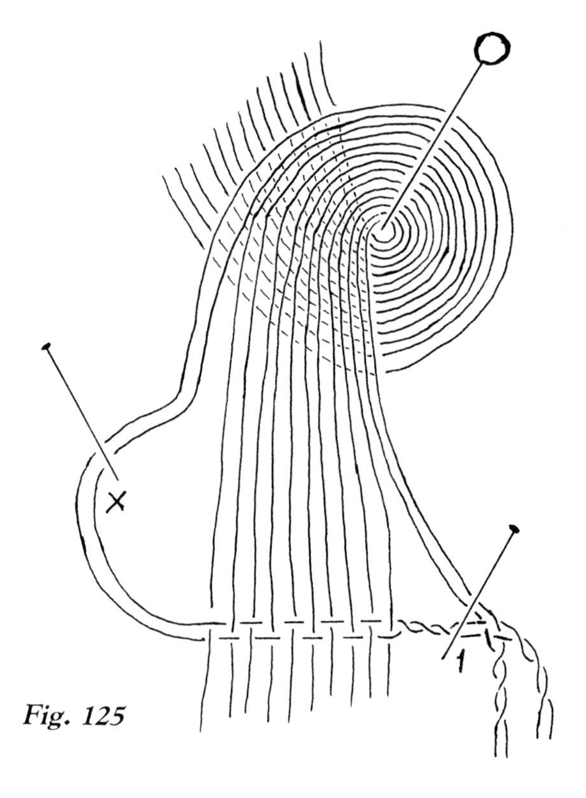

Fig. 125

last pair, make the turning stitch and rib to 9, leaving the rib after the edge stitch has been made.

Make the leadwork, twisting the pairs left out for it on each side four times before and after. Return to the ribs, taking in the leadwork pairs after 10 and 11 (take in first the pair that does not contain the weaver of the leadwork). To do this, simply work the runners through the leadwork pair at the end of the row of rib, make the turning stitch and work back to the pinhole side without attempting to pull up. Then, before making the purl (or the edge stitch, if working the left rib), pull up, holding the runners in the direction in which they are travelling. Meanwhile, with the other hand, pull up first the downright pair next to the leadwork pair, then the other downright pairs and *lastly* the leadwork pair. If this is the pair with the weaver, pull the passive bobbin first, then the weaver. Leave both ribs at 12 and 13 (this last is not a purl but an ordinary edge stitch).

The downright threads of the two ribs are now crossed through each other in whole stitch (fig. 126) and pulled up carefully. Begin the ribs for the next ring using the

Fig. 126

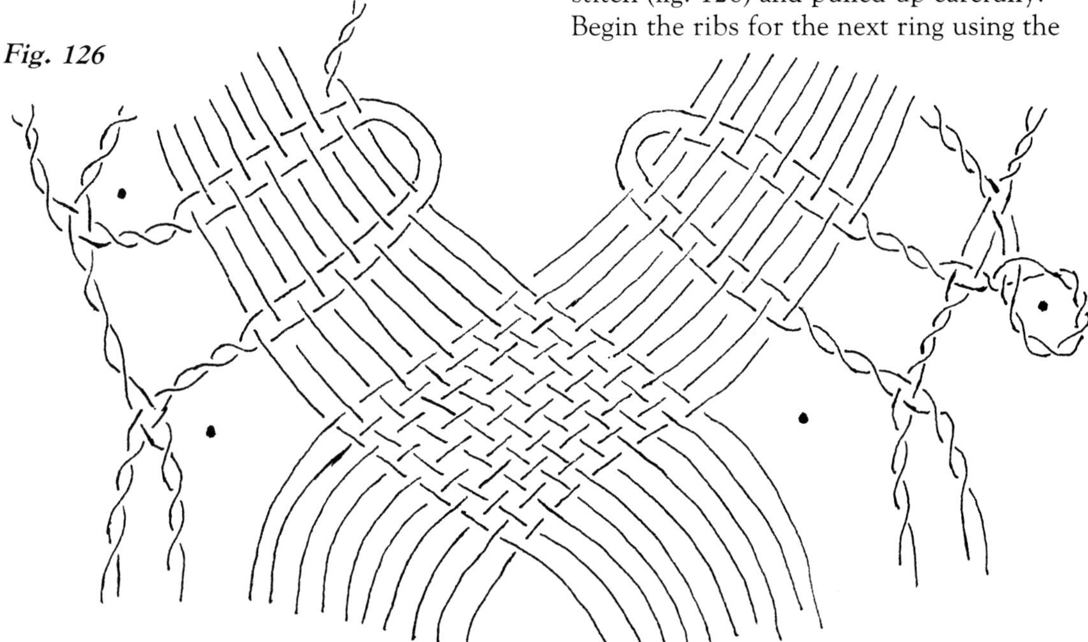

runners left at 12 and 13, reverting to making purls again on the right side. Note that the leadwork pairs are not left out or taken back into the ribs at the same places in each ring; as the rings are not all the same size or shape, this has to be left to the worker's judgement. Continue in this way all round the flower, crossing the downright threads between rings, as shown in fig. 126, and sewing out both ribs at the end into holes 1, 2 and 7 (fig. 124). One of the pairs from the last leadwork will probably have to be sewn out at 2 instead of being taken back into the rib. Tie, make two bunches and bow off. The threads of the outer bunch can be trimmed off short, but leave the threads of the inner bunch, pushing them out of the way under the cover cloth or slider until the filling and half stitch backing have been completed.

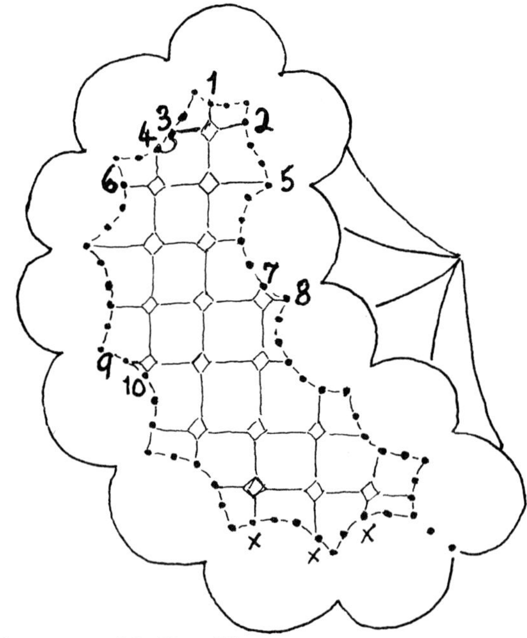

Fig. 127 *No Pin filling*

No Pin filling

This is worked more widely spaced than is usual (the pairs being sewn in 4 mm apart), and is subsequently backed by half stitch. No Pin is another variety of swing filling and the general working method has already been described under Devonshire Cutwork (*see* pp. 34–6). The differences are that in No Pin a leadwork is made with every vertical pair, and every row is a leadwork row. As before, there are three twists between leadworks, and the same weaver weaves all the leadworks in a row. Sew in one pair at 1 (fig. 127) and one pair at 2, and twist both pairs three times. Choosing the knot-free bobbin from 2 as weaver, make the leadwork, twist both pairs three times and top-sew the left pair, which contains the weaver, at 3. Tie this pair once, twist it twice, sew it in again at 4, twist it three times and leave it hanging as a vertical pair for the next row. Sew in a new pair at 5 and work the next row. Top-sew the pair containing the weaver at 6, pulling it up very carefully and tying it three times. This pair may now be left at the back or be bowed off, leaving the ends about 5 cm (2 in.) long. *These must not be trimmed off* until after the half stitch has been worked over the top of the filling.

Continue the filling, sewing in new pairs on the right side and sewing out on the left, as shown in fig. 127. You will find that while one row is being woven, the leadworks in the previous row move out of position in rather a disconcerting way – do not worry as the whole thing 'swings' back into shape at the end of the row, when the horizontal pair is being sewn out! The new pairs sewn in at 7 and 8 are each twisted only once before making the leadwork very close to the braid. The last leadwork in the following row is also made very close to the braid, after which the pairs are twisted once and sewn out at 9 and 10. When all the pairs have been sewn out and tied at the end, leave those that are hanging from the holes marked X – they can be used again for

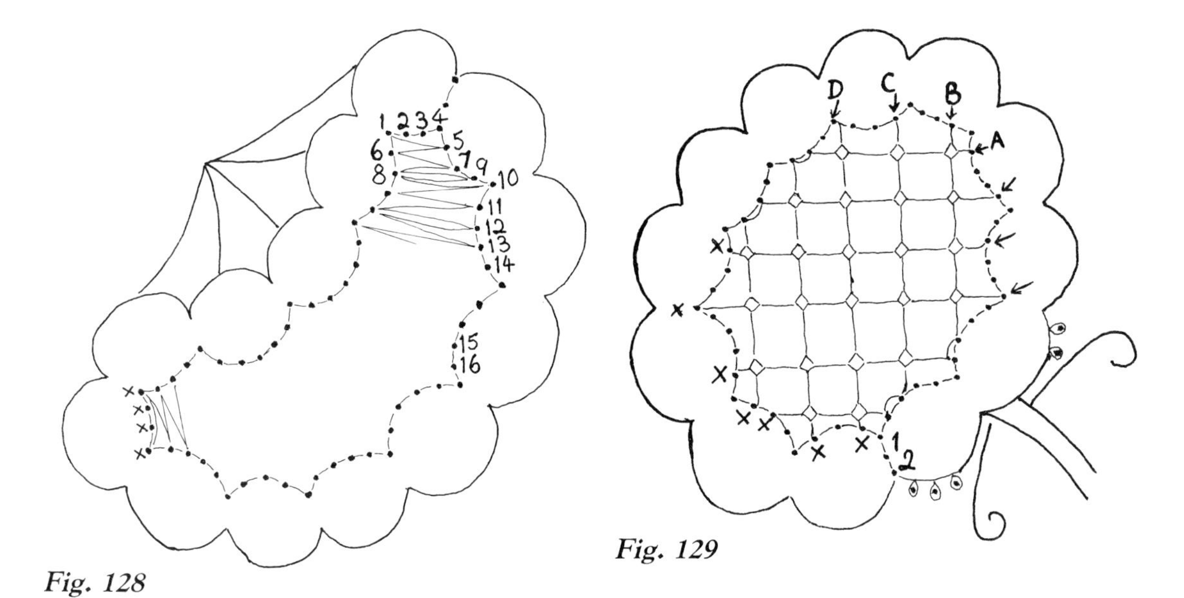

Fig. 128

Fig. 129

the half stitch backing. Bow off all other pairs, leaving long ends, and push these out of the way under a slider or cover cloth. Turn the pillow.

Half stitch backing

Sew one new pair into holes 1 and 3, and two each into holes 2 and 4 (fig. 128). Using the pair from 1 as runners, work a row of half stitch (making a whole stitch with the first and last pairs as usual), and sew the runners to the top bar of 5. Work to 6 and, before returning, sew a new pair to the lower bar of 5, laying this into the work as shown in fig. 56, p. 42. Work to 7 through all but the pair that is already hanging from this hole from the filling, which should be pushed to one side. Sew the runners at 7 and work back to 8. Before returning, lay the pair hanging from 7 into the work as above. Sew in a new pair at 9. Tie the runners at 10 and at all similar holes at the junction between rings on both sides. Take in the sewn-out filling pair at 11, sew in a new pair at 12 and 13, and take in the last of the sewn-out filling pairs at 14. Two more pairs were added at 15 and 16 (making fifteen pairs altogether) but, if a more open backing is desired, these last two pairs may be omitted.

On the other side it will be necessary to sew twice into the same hole occasionally, so that the weaving gradually changes direction and the sewing-out can be done in the narrowest part of the space at the end. When sewing into holes in which a pair has previously been sewn out from the filling, simply lift the thread ends out of the way if they interfere with the work. Begin to discard pairs in the last few rows, leaving seven or eight pairs to be sewn out into the holes marked X. These pairs are bowed off after tying – they should not be bunched. All the thread ends can now be trimmed off.

The other flower is made in the same way, holes 1 and 2 in fig. 129 corresponding with the same numbers in fig. 124. Note that in the last two rings of the round, only the encircled holes are used for purls – the remaining outer holes are used to make an ordinary pinhole edge. Fig. 129 also shows

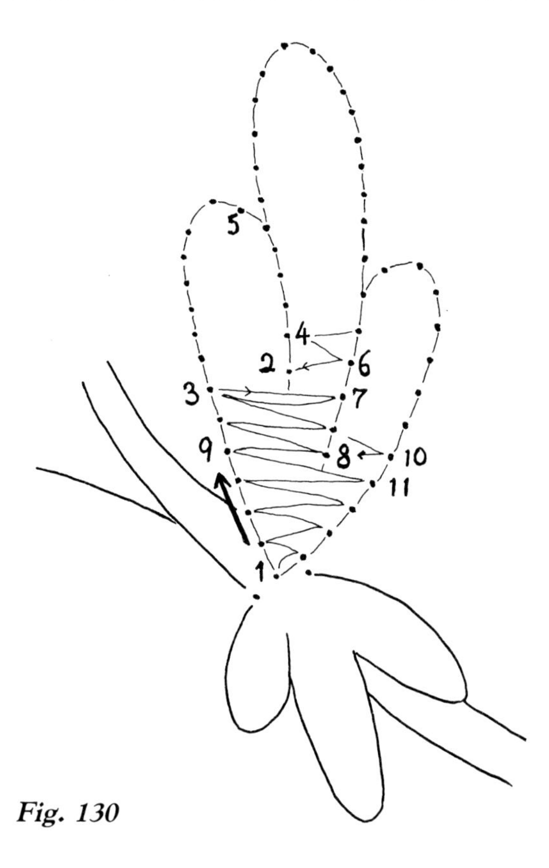

Fig. 130

where to sew in (arrowed holes) and sew out (holes marked X) the pairs for the filling. The first row is made with pairs sewn in at A, B, C and D. All but the first pair to be sewn out can be used again for the half stitch backing. This flower will take twenty pairs by the time the widest part of the space is reached, new pairs being added on both sides as the space widens.

When so many pairs are in use, it behoves the lacemaker to be particularly careful that no mistakes occur in the half stitch, and to stop and level the bobbins more often than is normally necessary. Bobbins hanging at different levels are frequently the cause of pairs becoming untwisted or double-twisted.

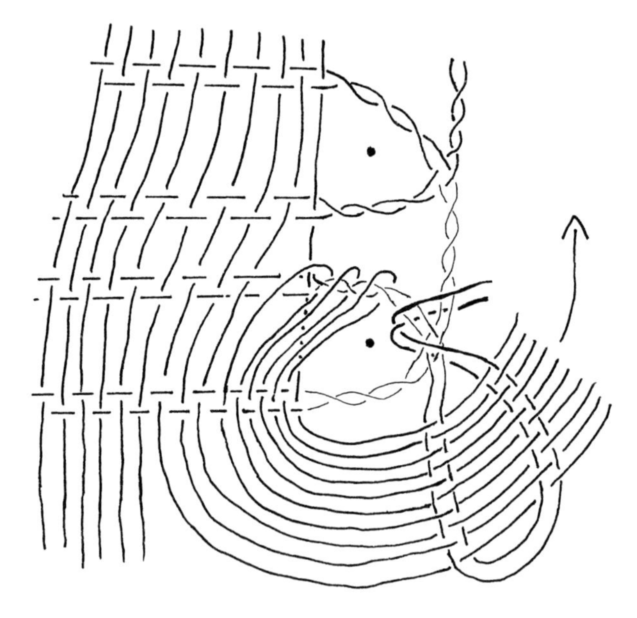

Fig. 131 *Beginning a rib in the middle of clothwork*

Leaf with raised lobes

This is the larger of the two leaflets to the right of the flower just made. Set up at 1 (fig. 130) with seven pairs and a magic thread, and rib up the side of the tap, pinholes on the right, in the direction of the arrow. Hang in and lay back four more pairs across the top and work back down the tap as usual, as far as the last hole on the pinhole side (hole 2). Hang in three new pairs here, laying these down inside the first downright thread. Make the edge stitch, work across to the other side, sew the runners to the upper bar of 3 and leave them there.

Now begin the rib for the middle tap. Untwist the edge pair at 2 and use it as runners to work through the next five downright pairs. Make a turning stitch, work back through these pairs and make an edge sewing at 2. The pin may be removed to make this sewing, but it is in fact easier to sew with the pin *in situ* (fig. 131). Push all but these six pairs well out of the way. Work another row of rib with the sewn runners, making the next sewing at 4. Continue the rib up the side of the tap, as in the petals of the Cone Flower (pattern 4), sewing in an edge pair at 5 and hanging in and laying back five more pairs round the top. Work back down the tap, arranging the rows so that from 6 the runners will work to 2. Sew the runners here with an edge sewing, inserting the needlepin into the braid hole and bringing it out under all the pairs that were turned here to make the rib. Tie the sewn pair once and leave it to become a downright pair. Replace pin 2.

The work continues with the runners that were left at 3. Straighten the pairs pushed aside from the first tap, and lay them in front of you so that the two sets lie side by side with the sewn pair hanging from 2 between them. With the runners from 3 work through all downright pairs to 7 and make the edge stitch. On returning, top-sew the runners to the lower bar of 3 to level the work. Discard one pair on the left side in each of the next two rows, hang in one new pair at 8 (as the clothwork is already so thick here, one pair is all that is necessary), work to 9 and leave the runners here after sewing them to the upper bar of this hole.

Make the rib for the last tap as before, using the edge pair from 8 and the next five downright pairs, and hanging in four more pairs round the top. Work back down the tap, arranging the rows so that from 10 the runners will work to 8, where they are sewn, tied and left hanging. The runner pair left at 9 now works across both sets to 11. Complete the leaf, throwing out pairs from both sides (and from the middle, in the last few rows), to reduce to about seven pairs at the end. After sewing to 1 (using the magic thread), tie the sewn pair twice, lay the remaining bobbins between the bobbins of the tied pair, and tie this again twice over

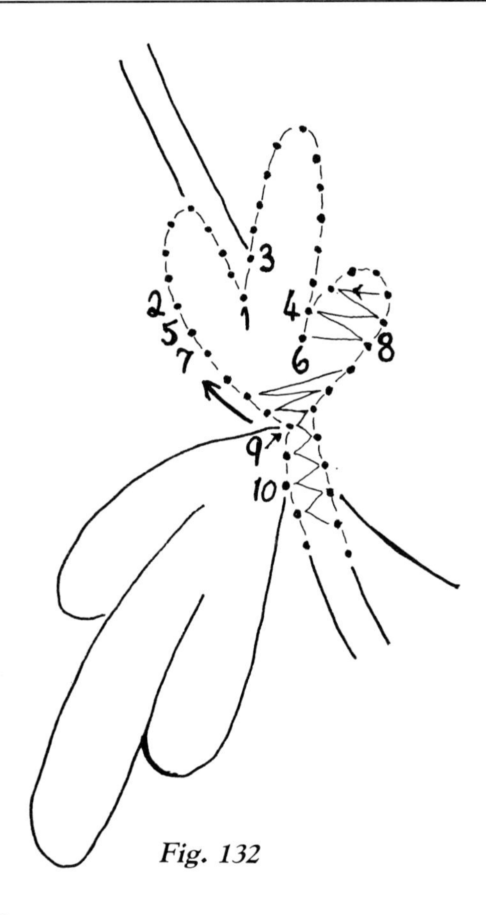

Fig. 132

the bunch. If more than seven pairs remain, cut out any surplus pairs from the bunch now. Leaving the bunch hanging, bow off and trim short all discarded threads.

Using the tied pair as an edge pair, and any pair out of the bunch as runners, begin the rib up the side of the smaller leaf, following the direction of the arrow in fig. 132 and hanging in and laying back three more pairs at the top. Work back down the tap. Before making the edge stitch at 1, hang in three new pairs, which are brought round the pin and laid down inside the first downright thread, and also one additional pair, which is slid up the runners and laid to the back of the pillow. Make the edge stitch and work to 2, sewing the runners to the lower bar if the upper bar of this hole has already been used. Leave the runners.

As before, untwist the edge pair, work it through the next five pairs, turn, work back and sew the runners at 1. Work another row of rib to 3, where an edge stitch is made with the pair which was laid to the back of the pillow, and which has first been twisted three times. Add two pairs at the top of this tap and work back down to 4. Begin a back stitch here, then work to 1, sew, tie and leave the runners. Work the runners left at 2 through all downright pairs, to make up the back stitch at 4. Work to 5, then to 6, where three new pairs are hung in, then work back and leave the runners after sewing them at 7.

Begin the rib for the last lobe as before, sewing into 6 and 4,then sewing in a new edge pair. Three new pairs are added across the top. Note that in this lobe the rows of whole stitch must be worked at a slight angle (see the course marked out for the runners in fig. 132), so that from a back stitch begun at 8 the runners will work to 6. Before working across with the runners from 7 to make up the back stitch, discard a pair on both sides, then continue to throw out a pair from each end in each row and some from the middle in the last few rows, so that by the time 9 is reached, only about eight or nine pairs remain. The sewing at 9 is best done without removing the pin.

The stem leading to the upper flower is started with the remaining pairs. Lay back a single bobbin from the downrights and replace it with a bobbin wound with coarse thread, tied to a pin higher up in the lace, which is laid down inside the edge pair (as third bobbin on the right). With the sewn runners from 9 continue the weaving, making edge stitches on the right. On the left, sew into the next two holes of the larger leaf but, before working to the second of these, discard another single bobbin and add another coarse thread to be the outermost downright bobbin on the left. Work to 10, sew the runners, work back and, before returning, sew in a new pair at 10 as an edge pair. Work up the stem, reducing to eight pairs as it narrows.

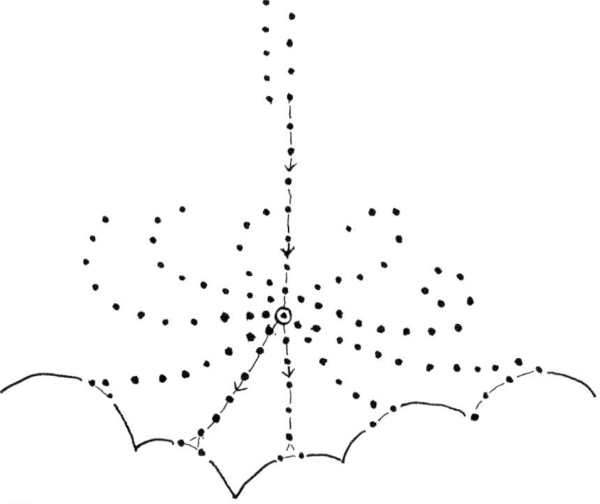

Fig. 133

Near the top, the braid changes to rib. After making the last pinhole on the left side, throw back the coarse threads, work to the other side and hang in a new pair before making the edge stitch. Continue in rib with these eight pairs, following the arrowed line in fig. 133. The rib divides into two; after making the ringed hole, work to the plain side, make the turning stitch and work back through one more pair. Twist the runners three times, set a pin under them into the first hole of the left branch, and make an edge stitch with the next downright pair, which has first been twisted three times. These four pairs work the left branch and are sewn out into the flower. These are top sewings round the three-twist bars below the purl loops (fig. 134) and, in order to bring the weaving right up to these places, it will be necessary to work two or three rows without pins, using the method shown in fig. 109, p. 76, before sewing out. Raise but do not remove the purl pins whilst sewing. Tie and bunch the pairs and bow off.

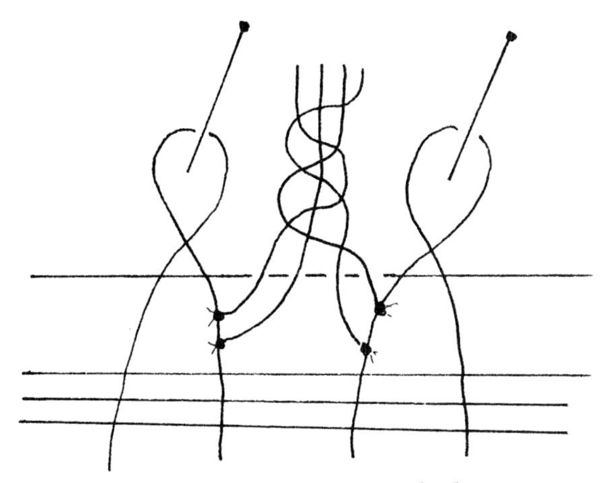

Fig. 134 Sewing out into a purl edge

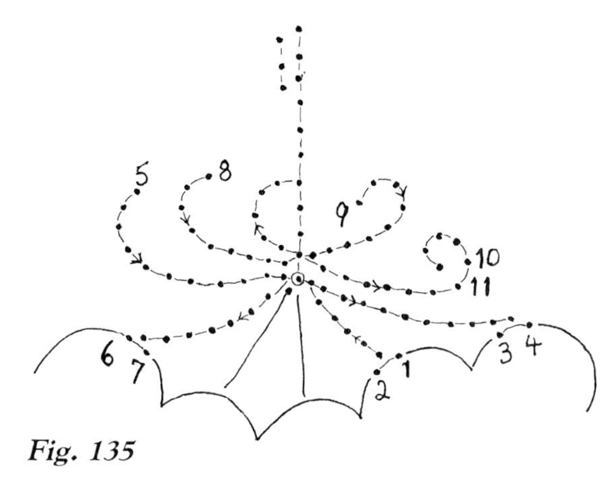

Fig. 135

Return to the four pairs that were left at the ringed hole. Using the outer left downright pair as runners, work them to the right to make the first hole of the rib on the right of the completed rib. Finish this rib and sew out as before.

Sew in two pairs each at 1 and 2 (fig. 135), again round the three-twist bars below the purl loops. Work two or three rows without pins to bring the threads close to the first hole of the rib, then rib down the arrowed line (pinholes on the right).

When the pin has been set into the last hole before the ringed hole, make a whole stitch with the edge pair, but do not twist either pair. Sew the right of these two pairs to the ringed hole with an edge sewing, tie it once and leave it. Turn the pillow in preparation for making the next rib. Give three twists to the outer pair on the left. Take the next pair (second pair from the left) and whole-stitch it through two pairs to the right. Make the turning stitch, work back, set the first pin of the next rib and make the edge stitch with the twisted pair. Continue the rib and sew out into the flower at 3 and 4, as before.

Set up with four pairs at 5 and rib towards the stem, pinholes on the left. **After the last hole before the stem, work to the plain side and top-sew the runners to the ringed hole. Replace the pin. Make a whole stitch with the sewn runners and the next pair, top-sew this pair to the first hole of the first rib made, twist it three times and leave it. Turn the pillow.

Untwist the outer pair on the left (the old edge pair) and use it as runners to work to the right, to the first hole of the next rib, making the edge stitch with the newly twisted pair**. This rib finishes at 6 and 7.

Set up again at 8 with four pairs and rib towards the stem, pinholes on the left. The turn into the next rib is made as before – follow instructions from * to *, except for making the sewing a top sewing into the hole below the ringed hole, and reading 'right' for 'left', and vice versa. The following rib is sewn out with top sewings into the stem.

The last pair of ribs is started at 9, and the turn at the stem is made following instructions from ** to **, except that of the two sewings the first is an edge sewing into the hole below the ringed hole, and the second is made into the ringed hole; again, read 'right' for 'left', and vice versa. When the last hole of the second rib has been made, work to the plain side, top-sewing the runners to 10 and the edge pair to 11.

Tie and bunch and, after tying the outside pairs over the bunch, spread the two unsewn pairs apart to make the knots ride up as much as possible. Cut off.

Half stitch leaf with raised lobes

Make the centre leaflet first, setting up at 1 (fig. 136) with seven pairs and a magic thread. Rib in the direction of the arrow, hanging in and laying back one pair at 2, and laying back a pair from the rib at 3 and 4. Rib to 5 and turn. Work back the tap as usual in half stitch, following the course of the runners drawn on the diagram. Before making the edge stitch at 6 hang in three pairs, laying down each pair inside the first downright thread, and each time giving a twist to the right bobbin of the new pair and the next bobbin on its right. Work to 7, sew the runners and leave. The rib for the next lobe is made as in the whole stitch leaf, using the edge pair and the next five pairs and sewing in a new pair at 5 as an edge pair.

Hang in and lay back two pairs at the top, and work back down the tap in half stitch, following the course of the runners shown on the diagram. From 8 work to 6, sew in the runners, tie them once and leave them. (Do *not* twist this pair, or the whole stitch pair on its left, before working the next row.) Bring down the pairs pushed aside from the first tap and lay them straight, checking that each pair except the whole stitch pair on the right still has one twist.

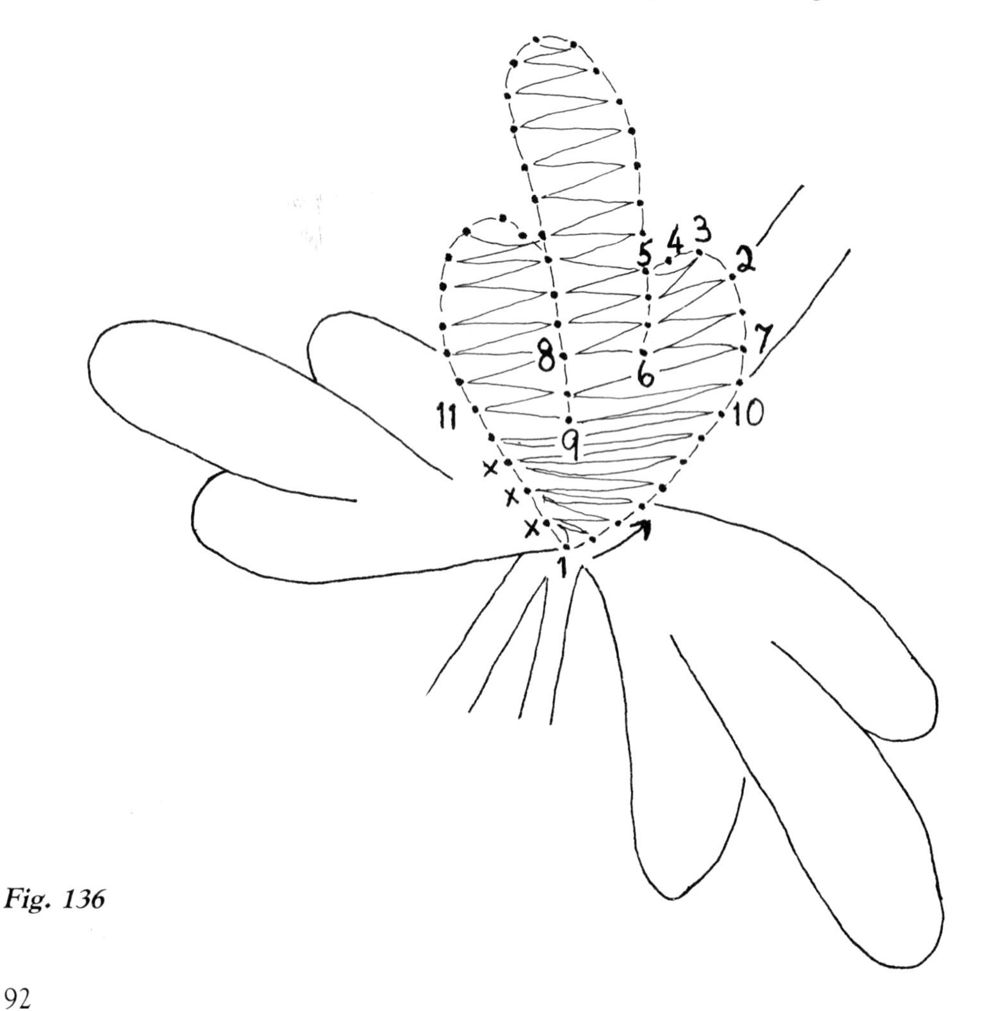

Fig. 136

Work across both sets to the hole below 8, using the runners left at 7. Continue working with all fourteen pairs until 9 is reached, where three more pairs are hung in as before. Work to 10, sew in the runners and leave them.

Work the rib and last lobe similarly, hanging in and laying back two new pairs at the top. Join up both sets as before, working the runners from 11 to 9, sewing and leaving them there, then working across both sets with the runners waiting at 10. Begin throwing out pairs immediately from both ends of each row, and make back stitches at holes marked X in order to be level by the time the end of the leaflet is reached. Sew the runners at 1, using the magic thread, and tie them once. There should be six pairs left at this stage; do not cut these off. Trim off all discarded pairs and tidy the pins.

The remaining six pairs make the rib up the side of the next leaflet. Untwist the edge pair at 1 (fig. 137), use it as runners to work through the other five pairs, make a turning stitch and work back, sewing the runners at 1. Continue the rib in the direction of the arrow, making edge sewings to the side of the completed leaflet and sewing in an edge pair where the two leaflets diverge. Hang in two pairs across the top and work back, discarding two pairs on the rib side before 2

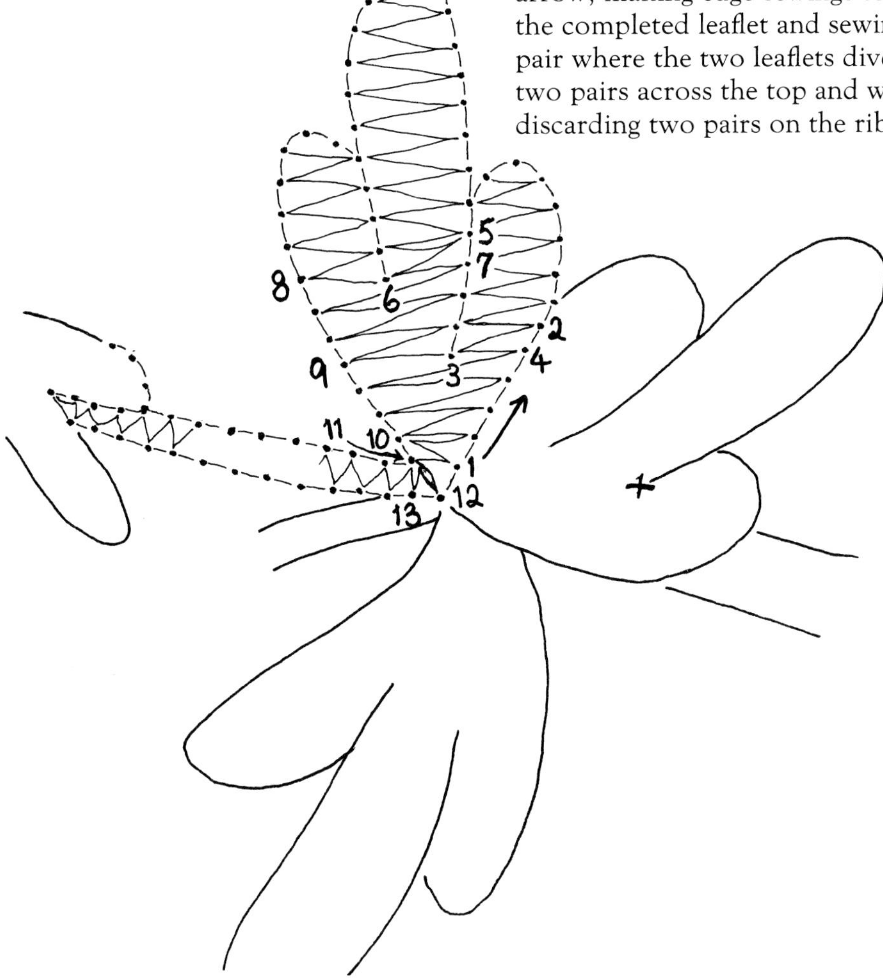

Fig. 137

is reached. From here work to 3, hang in three new pairs, work to 4, sew the runners and leave them.

Make the rib for the middle lobe, again hanging in two new pairs at the top. Work back, arranging the rows so that from 5 the runners will work to 6, where two new pairs are added. Work to 7, sew the runners and leave them.

Make the rib for the third lobe, hanging in and laying back one new pair at the top, and work back. From 8 work to 6, sew the runners, tie and leave them. Bring down and lay straight the bobbins of the middle lobe, and use the runner pair left at 7 to work across both sets to the hole below 8. Discard three pairs before 9 is reached, leaving ten pairs. From 9 work to 3, sew and tie the runners and leave them. Bring down and lay straight the pairs from the first lobe, and continue the leaflet with the runners left at 4, discarding pairs from both sides until eight pairs remain at the end. Make a back stitch at 10. Begin a back stitch at 11, work to 12 and sew the runners. Although it is now fairly safe to remove the pin for the sewing, as the pinhole has already been used once, it is better to make this sewing without removing the pin. Make a whole stitch with the sewn pair and the next pair, and sew this pair also to 12, then twist it three times.

The pairs are now used to make the stem to the whole stitch leaf. Tie two coarse threads to a pin at about X, and lay these bobbins between pins 11 and 12 as the third bobbin on the left and the fifth bobbin on the right. Change to whole stitch. Using the second pair from the right (the untwisted pair of the two sewn at 12) as runners, work them through the coarse pair, tie them once, then work them through four more pairs, leaving them lying inside the coarse pair on the other side. Use the last pair they passed

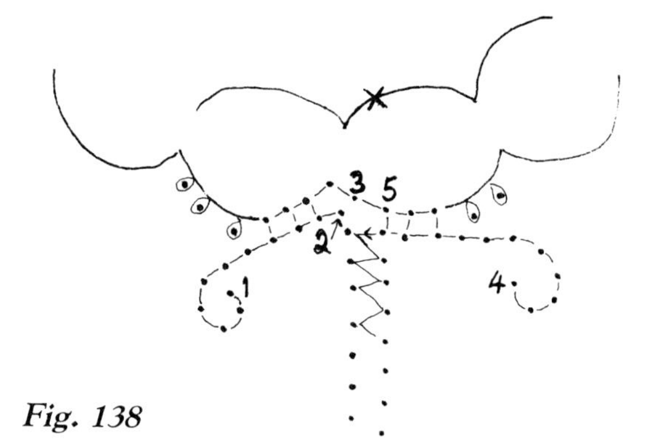

Fig. 138

through as new runners and work back, making the edge stitch at 13 with the twisted pair hanging from 12. Work back, and make up the back stitch at 11.

Make the stem. Sew out the left edge pair where it touches the leaflet and, after another row, throw out the left coarse pair. Continue, making top sewings on the left and throwing back pairs as the stem narrows. Sew out the last few pairs – these do not need to be bunched before bowing off.

Set up again at 1 (fig. 138) to work the little four-pair rib, pinholes on the right, under the lower flower. Where this rib runs beside the edge of the flower make joins (*see* Glossary, *Sewing to Join Two Edges*). After making the edge stitch and three twists at 2, work the runners to the plain side, twist them three times and leave them to become an edge pair for the stalk. Sew the edge pair on the right to 3, work this pair through two pairs to the left and leave it. Make a whole stitch with the remaining two pairs, discard the left pair, sew the right pair to 3, tie it once and leave it. These three pairs are laid aside and will be used for the stalk.

Make the little rib on the other side, setting up at 4 and again making joins to the flower where shown on the diagram. After the join to 5, work back to the plain side, twist the runners three times and leave them to become an edge pair. Untwist the edge pair on the left, sew it also to 5, use it to make a whole stitch with the next pair, then sew this pair to 3. Turn the pillow so that the stalk faces you.

Bring down the three pairs left waiting from the other rib, and lay them straight, beside the four pairs in use. Tie two coarse threads to a pin at about X, and lay these in position as fifth bobbin from the right and third bobbin from the left. The second pair from the right are the runners. Make the stalk, joining to the tip of the leaflet where this touches.

At 1 (fig. 139) make a join to 2, as above, work back to the other side and, before returning, sew out the right edge pair with a top sewing to the lower bar of 2. Continue

Fig. 139

the stalk, making top sewings on the right. After sewing at 3 (this is an edge sewing and the pin can now safely be removed to make it), throw back the coarse threads. The right-hand coarse thread can be cut off short, but leave an end to the left one and do not trim it off until the leaflet is finished. From 3 work the runners through one pair, tie them once, then work through the remaining four pairs, make a turning stitch, work back and sew to 4. Continue the rib up the side of the leaflet, sewing in an edge pair at 5.

This leaflet is made in the same way as the previous ones. One pair was added at the top of the first lobe and two each at the tops of the second and third. Discard two pairs on the right side where this last lobe narrows, before the two sets are joined, and continue to throw out pairs after the joining from both sides, so that only five or six pairs are left to sew out at the end.

For the cut end of the stalk set up at 1 (fig. 140) with eight pairs and a coarse pair. Hang in two pairs each at 2 and 3, and one pair at 4. Remember to tie the runners at 4. Work in whole stitch and sew out into the leaf.

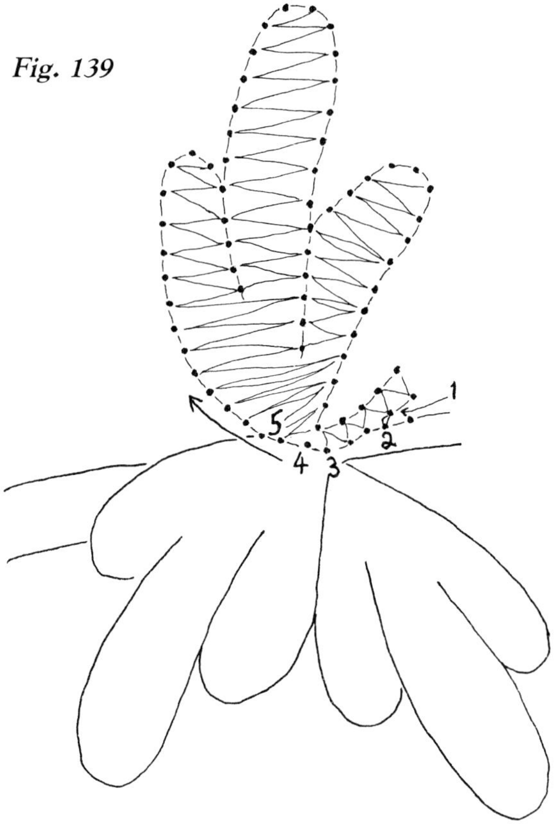

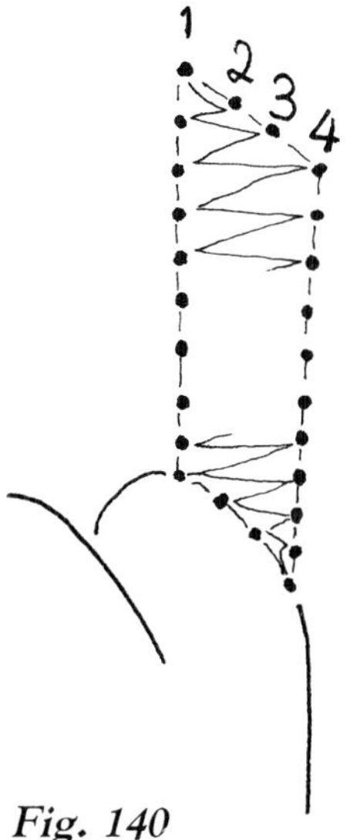

Fig. 140

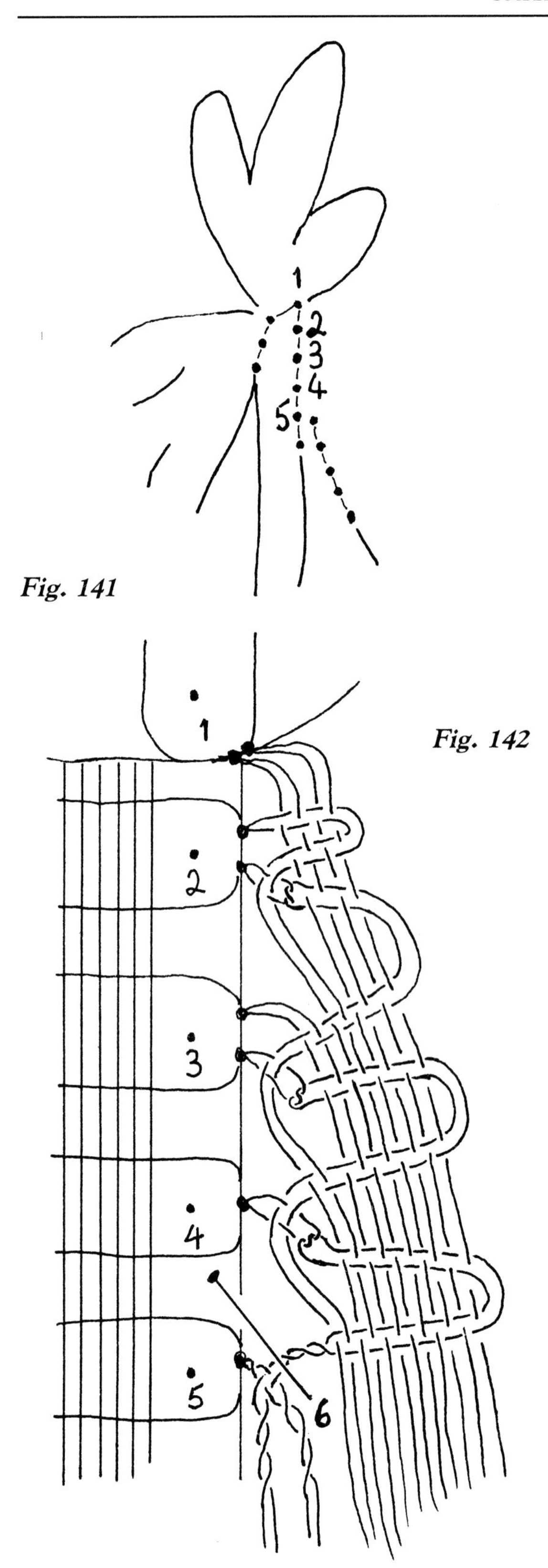

Fig. 141

Fig. 142

The stalk leading to the single leaflet at the top is made next. Sew in two pairs each at 1, 2 and 3 (fig. 141), and one pair each at 4 and 5. With the third pair from the right (fig. 142), work in whole stitch through the two pairs from 1, make a turning stitch and work back, this time going through the other pair from 2. Leave the runners, tie the last pair they passed through once and use it as new runners to work another row of rib, this time taking in both pairs from 3. Again, leave the runners, tie the last pair through which they passed, and work with it to the plain side and back, going through the pair from 4. This pair in turn becomes a runner pair but, on returning from the plain side through the downright pairs, twist it three times, set pin 6 under it and make an edge stitch with the pair from 5, which has first been twisted. At 1 (fig. 143) hang in and lay aside to the right two new pairs, one before and one after making the edge stitch; also lay a pair out of the rib, placing it between them. Work three or four more holes of rib with the seven remaining pairs, then leave these bobbins and turn the pillow.

Caterpillar

Place the three pairs laid aside at 1 in front of you. Thread a pair wound with coarse thread through the middle pair of the three (under one bobbin and over the other) and lay the coarse threads to the back of the pillow. Give three twists to the left of the three pairs in front of you. With the other two pairs make a whole stitch, twist the left of these three times and set pin 2 under it. Hang in two new pairs, placing these between the bobbins of the untwisted pair. Make the edge stitch at 2 with the twisted pairs. Bring down the coarse threads to lie as first bobbin on the right and fifth bobbin on the left (taking care that this thread is not hooked round the outside of pin 2).

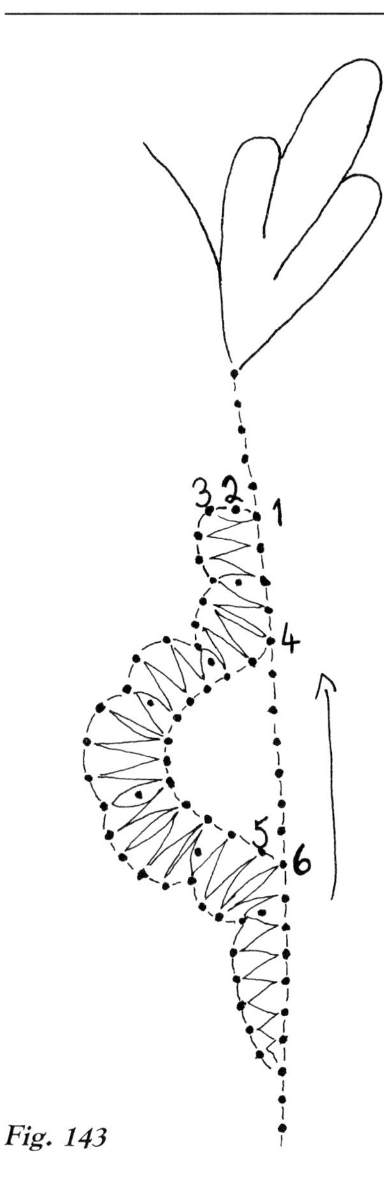

Fig. 143

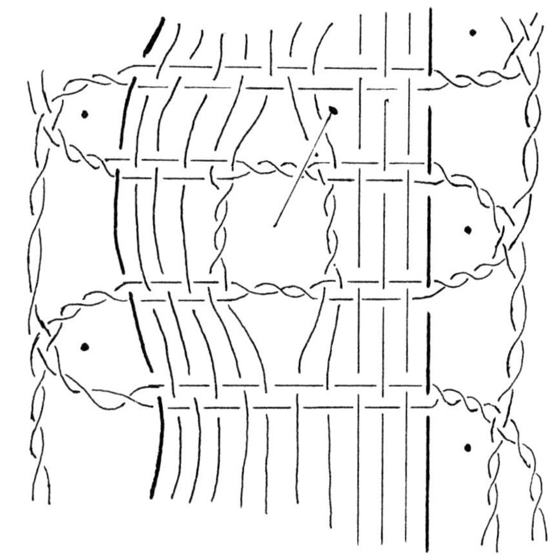

Fig. 144

Work back through the coarse pair, tie the runners, work them through one more pair and leave them. With the last pair they passed and the neighbouring coarse pair, make a whole stitch, twist the left of these pairs three times and set pin 3 under it. Again, hang in two new pairs, placing these inside the coarse thread as usual, make up the edge and work back through all pairs, remembering to tie the runners after the first stitch. Top-sew the runners to the lower bar of 1. In the return row begin a hole in the middle (*see* fig. 144, showing the hole with a pinhole edge instead of sewings on the right-hand side). These holes are made in the middle of each segment, but are not shown on the pricking to avoid confusion with the holes that mark the places where the coarse thread is crossed between the segments. It is therefore best to prick the pinhole for each hole in the braid, when this point is reached.

Continue the braid, crossing the left coarse thread where indicated and following the course of the runners drawn on the diagram. Tie the runners when they have passed back through the coarse pair after the sewing at 4, and also sew in an edge pair round the lower bar of 4. Tie the runners again after 5 and sew out the edge pair at 6, thereafter making top sewings on the right side. Reduce the number of pairs and sew out the last few into the stalk. Bunch, and tie back the little bunch, using two of the discarded pairs.

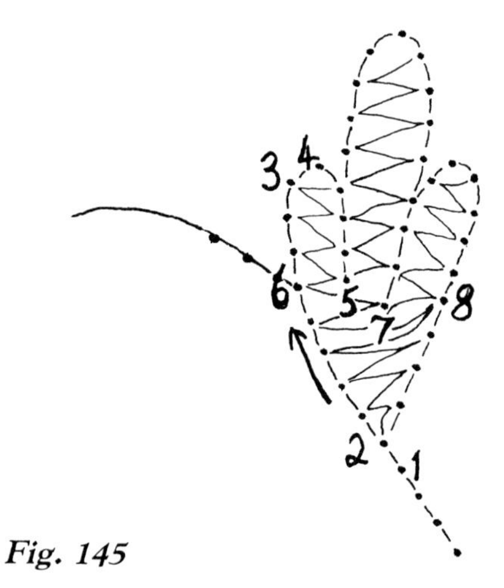

Fig. 145

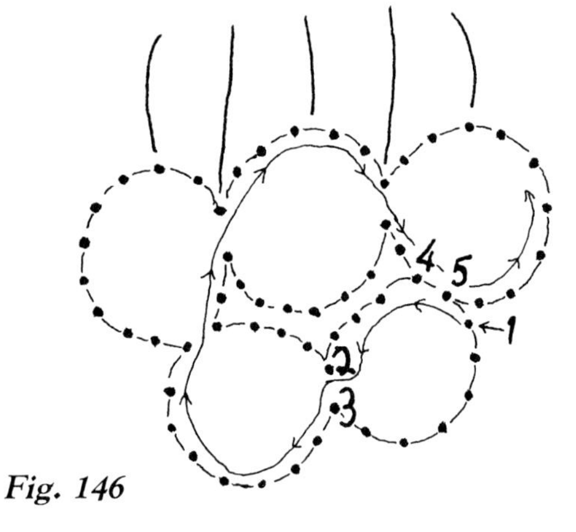

Fig. 146

Return to the rib pairs. After making the edge stitch at 1 (fig. 145), give three twists to the outer pair on the right and make the next hole at 2 on the right side of the rib. Continue the rib with holes on the right up the side of the top leaf.

This leaf is made like the others, except that the inner raised ridges are rolled and not ribbed. Work the first tap with seven pairs – lay back a pair from the rib at 3 and 4 – as far as 5. Then hang in three pairs, which are laid down inside the first downright thread as usual, and one extra pair, which is laid to the back of the pillow. Make up the edge, work to 6, sew and leave the runners.

Now make the roll, winding the edge pair at 5 round and round the next five downright pairs until the roll is long enough to reach to 4. Here the winding pair is sewn in, tied twice, twisted and left to become the edge pair. The pair that was hung in and laid back at 5 is used to attach the roll, the first sewing being made into the hole above 5. Continue the rib to the top of the lobe, hanging in two new pairs at the top. All these pairs remain in the work, and so the clothwork will be thick enough when 7 is reached to hang in only one new pair, which is laid into the work, and one extra pair, which is laid back for attaching the next roll.

One new pair is hung in at the top of the last lobe. Work back down this lobe and begin a back stitch at 8 before working to 7, sewing and leaving the runners. Make up the back stitch with the sewn runner pair from the other side. At the end, sew out into hole 2 and tie back the little bunch of threads.

The bud

Set up at 1 (fig. 146) with seven pairs and a magic thread, and rib with pinholes on the left in the direction of the arrows. After the edge stitch at 2 change the pinhole side, i.e. give three twists to the outer pair on the right, work through and make the next edge stitch at 3 with this twisted pair. Continue the rib, as shown on the diagram, changing the side on which the pinholes are made, as above, every time the rib passes between two holes from one ring into the next, and remembering to tie the runners occasionally on the outer curves.

Having made the hole before 4, work to the plain side and leave the runners. Sew the left edge pair to 4, twist it three times, sew

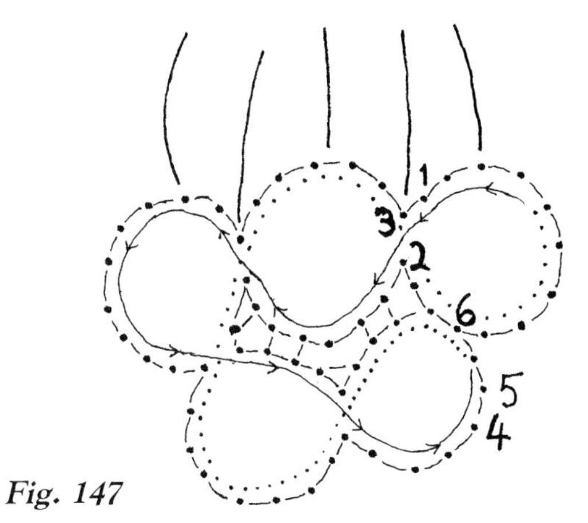

Fig. 147

it to 5 and twist it three times again (edge sewings). Continue the rib with the runners left on the plain side, making edge sewings at 4 and 5 over both the edge and the sewn pair, then going on with edge stitches again round the rest of this ring.

Use edge sewings to cross the ribs. After 1 (fig. 147) work to the plain side, sew the runners to 2, twist them three times and leave them to become an edge pair. Sew the next downright pair also to 2. Sew the edge pair on the other side to 3 – this now becomes a downright pair. Continue the rib, using the sewn downright pair from 2 as runners, working it first to the plain side on the left, and making pinholes on the right.

At the next two holes of this section join to the neighbouring rib (*see* Glossary, *Sewing to Join Two Edges*). More of these joins are indicated on the diagram wherever the rib being made comes close to a completed part. Do not omit these, as they keep the rings in shape when the pins are removed. Continue round the rings in the direction of the arrows, sewing and changing the pinhole side where the ribs cross.

When joining to the starting point, the pairs may be spread a little so that they can all be used again for the half stitch backing. At each of the last two holes (4 and 5) lay out a pair from the rib, pushing these to the right of the pillow. From 5 work to the plain side and sew the runners to the starting hole, using the magic thread. Tie this pair twice. Lay the first two downright pairs on the right next to the two pairs already laid aside. Lay the sewn runners next to these. Sew the next (and last) downright pair to the starting hole and lay it beside the others. Sew the edge pair to the starting hole, tie it twice, twist it three times and top-sew it to the nearest bar of the next hole at 6. Lay this pair also beside the others. All seven pairs are now ready to be used for the filling. Lay them aside, keeping them in order. Remove all pins from the middle of the bud, leaving the pins round the outline.

For the half stitch filling top-sew one pair at 1 (fig. 148), two pairs at 2, 3 and 4, and one pair at 5. Work with these eight pairs, using the pair from 1 as runners and following the course drawn for the runners on the diagram. From 6 work through all the pairs in use, making a half stitch with the whole stitch pair at the end of the row, then making a whole stitch with the pair hanging from 7 (the nearest of the pairs that were laid aside). Leave the runners, tie the pair from 7 and use it as runners to work to 8. In the next row the runners work through

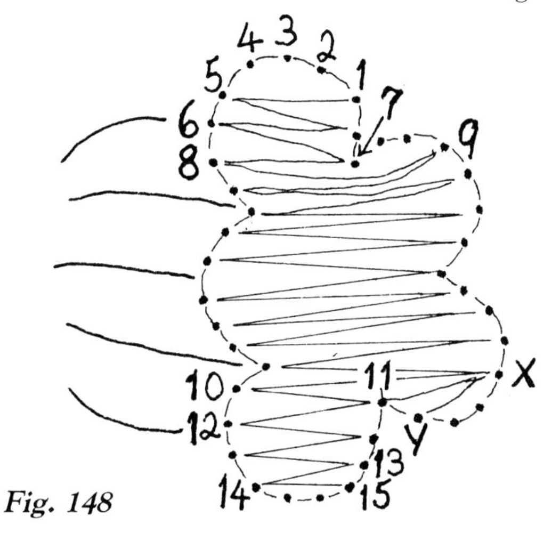

Fig. 148

all pairs, including the rest of those that were laid aside, making a whole stitch with the last pair hanging at 9. Tie this pair and use it as runners for the next row. From now on the work proceeds normally. Here and there, when passing over the central ribs underneath, the runners should be sewn (fig. 50, p. 38), and four such sewings were made spaced out over the whole of the filling. Remember also to tie the runners at the outermost hole of each curve.

After 10 work through seven pairs, making a whole stitch with the last of these, then top-sew the runners to 11. Push the seven unworked pairs aside, work back to 12 with the sewn runners and continue to fill in this ring. Discard one pair at each end of the row, following the sewing at 13. From 14 work a final row in whole stitch and sew out the runners at 15. Take the second and third downright bobbins on one side, tie them three times and lay them back, leaving four pairs to be sewn out in the remaining two holes.

Seven pairs now remain to finish the other ring. Sew the outer pair on the left to 11 and use it as runners to work through the remaining pairs to X. After sewing here, work a final row in whole stitch and sew out the runners at Y. Tie and lay back the second and third downright bobbins on each side, and sew out the last four pairs in the two remaining holes. Bow off all pairs when they have been tied, and trim the ends short.

For the stalk, sew in three pairs each at 1 and 2 (fig. 149), and one pair at 3. Use the middle pair as runners, working with it through three pairs to the right; make a turning stitch and work back through all but the pair hanging from 3. Leave the runners, tie the last pair they passed and use it as runners to work another row of rib, making an edge stitch at 4, when returning

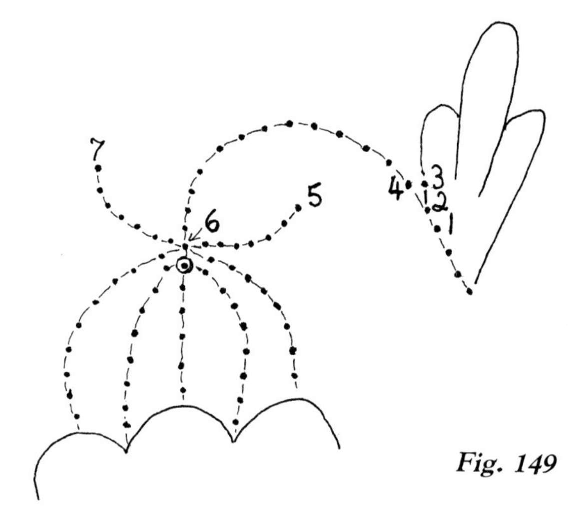

Fig. 149

to the left side, with the pair from 3. Continue the rib.

Before making the edge stitch at the ringed hole, hang in one pair, laying it inside the first downright thread, and two more pairs, which are laid out to the left back of the pillow. Make the edge stitch and hang two more pairs round the runners (second pair from the left), laying these out beside the other two. Push aside the first four downright pairs on the right of the rib, and complete the middle stalk with the four pairs left in front of you. Sew out into the bud. Work the ribs on each side of the centre stalk with the pairs left ready for them, and sew out into the bud.

Set up again with four pairs at 5 and rib towards the stem, pinholes on the right. After setting the last pin before the stem, work once more to the plain side and back, leaving the runners inside the unworked edge pair. Sew the outermost left downright pair to the right bar of 6, use it to make a whole stitch with the next pair, then sew this pair to the left bar of the ringed hole. Turn the pillow so that the next section of rib faces you. The runner pair (now second pair from the right) works through the two sewn pairs, makes a turning stitch and works back to make the first hole of the next section with the edge pair, which was left hanging. Complete the rib and sew out into the bud. Make the last rib, setting up at 7 and working as above, but reading 'left' for 'right', and vice versa.

Working Methods

Fillings backed with half stitch or whole stitch

Not every filling is suitable for backing. Avoid those that have a fine, net-like appearance, such as Four Pin or Italian, which would look very confused against the backing. Choose those with bold, well-defined spots with spaces between. A favourite filling for this treatment is Diamond, but Whole Stitch Block, Brick and Straight Pin also look effective.

Remember to remove any pins from the filling before embarking on the backing. Do not cut short any of the thread ends after sewing out the filling, until the backing has been completed. Occasionally a filling is backed with whole stitch, and in this case care should be taken to keep the backing thin and gauzy so that the filling will show up well against it.

No Pin filling

When this is made conventionally, the pairs are usually sewn in at every hole or every second hole along the edge of the braid, giving the filling a chequer-board appearance. However, when, as is the case in this pattern, the rows of filling are spread wider apart, it is best not to rely on one's judgement but to draw a grid, with the lines the required distance apart, either on the pricking itself (remember not to use pencil) or on a photocopy. This will show exactly where the pairs must be sewn in and out.

Leaves with raised lobes

Although frequently seen in older Honiton laces, this method of starting a rib in the middle of a piece of clothwork seems not to have been used much in recent years. This is mainly, I think, because such shapes would most likely be raised all round the outer edges as well. Thus a leaflet like the ones in this pattern would be ribbed up one side, round the top of the lobe and right to the bottom of the indentation; the pairs would then be rolled back and the rib continued right round the next lobe, etc., finishing up at the end of the leaf on the other side. At the same time, pairs would be hung in at the top of each lobe for filling in when the ribbing was completed.

However, the technique shown here also has its uses. The leaves in this design demonstrate that it works as well in half stitch as in whole stitch; that although it is more convenient to work the shallower indentations first, this is not essential and one can begin with a deeper indentation if necessary; that the internal ridge can be either ribbed or rolled; and that the pairs borrowed from the clothwork can be used to make a rib that is not attached to the previous lobe.

When using this technique there are one or two points to watch for. A careful eye should be kept on the angle at which each lobe is woven, so that, by the time the lobes are joined, the clothwork in each is being made at the same angle.

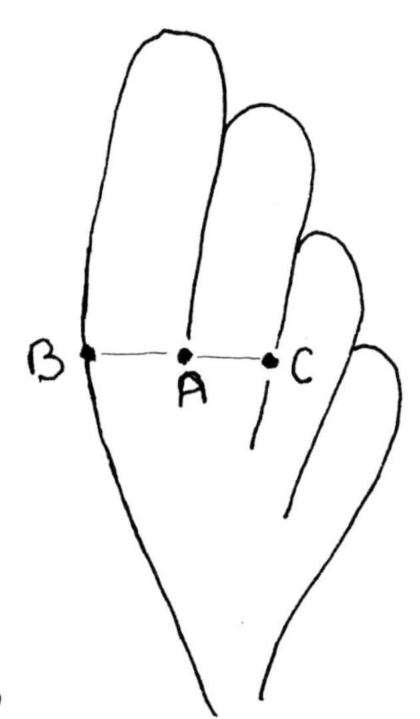

Fig. 150

When finishing a lobe, make sure that the hole at which the runners are abandoned – B in fig. 150 – is level with or very slightly above the level of A. The same holds good for hole C, the hole from which the runners of the next lobe work to A. If either B or C is much below the level of A, a gap may appear in the weaving when the two sets are joined together.

In order to get the weaving fairly level at this point, it may be necessary to use holes B or C twice. In the case of C the worker must look ahead – if a back stitch is necessary here, it must be begun before the runners work to A and are sewn and left.

How many new pairs are to be added at A before making the new rib or roll depends on the density of the existing clothwork and on how many pairs are required for the rib/roll. Here again, the decision rests with the worker. A. Penderel Moody, who first described this technique in her book *Devon Pillow Lace*, added no extra pairs at all, but the clothwork in the accompanying illustration appears to be very thick, and the little rib was made with only five pairs. If the worker has underestimated the number of pairs needed, and the clothwork looks a little thin below A when the two sets have been joined, it is always possible to sew in a new pair at A in addition to the old runner pair already hanging there. However, it is better to wait until two or three rows have been worked, as the threads tend to close up under A in a very satisfactory way and one may find that there was no need for the new pair after all.

The same technique may be used for making a tap leaf, when only a single ridge is wanted up the middle, like that shown in fig. 151. The advantage of using this method is that the whole leaf can be made in one piece without having to sew out at the end of the first half. The disadvantage is that the top of the first tap does not have a raised outline.

Fig. 151 (right) *Tap leaf with single ridge along centre vein*

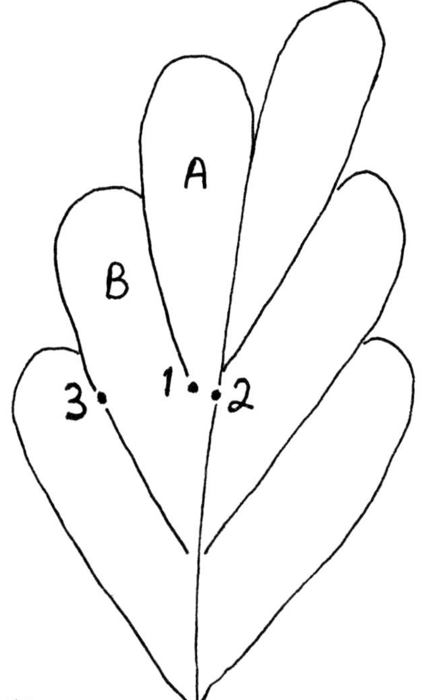

Fig. 152

Work tap A (fig.152) from the top as a flat leaf, making pinhole edges on both sides. Reduce the pairs at the bottom to the number needed for the rib/roll, plus four pairs (i.e. the edge pair and runners on the resting side, and two pairs to fill in the space between 1 and 2 when the two sets are joined). In the worked sample (fig. 151) this was ten pairs.

After hole 1, the last hole on the outer side of the tap, work to 2 on the mid-rib side. This hole should be more or less level with 1. Make the edge stitch. Push aside the runners and edge pair and the next two downright pairs. Use the remaining six pairs to rib up to the top of B (sewing in an edge pair where the taps diverge), as described in the pattern, or, if a roll is wanted, make it with these six pairs. Use one of the discarded pairs near the end of tap A to attach the roll.

When tap B has been made as far as the end of the roll, the runners are sewn to 1, tied once and left hanging. Bring down the pairs that were laid aside from the last tap and use the runners from 2 to work across all pairs to 3. Continue the tap, making a pinhole edge on both sides and again reducing to ten pairs at the end. When the last tap on this side has been made, reduce to what is needed for the rib or roll up the mid-rib. After the last hole, work the runners through all pairs, including the edge pair on the other side, tie the runners twice, lay all other pairs between these bobbins and tie them twice again over the bunch. Make the rib or roll to the top of the highest tap on the other side of the leaf. The taps on this side are then made in the conventional way, as described in pattern 2.

The pricking for fig. 151 has been included as fig. 153 to show that no adaptation is necessary when using this technique with other patterns. A double-ridged leaf like those described in pattern 2 could be made over the same pricking.

Fig. 153 *Pricking for tap leaf with single ridge along centre vein*

Bibliography

Historical

Bath, Virginia Churchill, *Lace*, Penguin Books, 1979

Earnshaw, Pat, *Identification of Lace*, Shire Publications, 1980 and *A Dictionary of Lace*, Shire Publications, 1982

Inder, P. M., *Honiton Lace*, Exeter Museum's Publication No. 55, revised 1977

Jackson, Mrs F. Nevill, *A History of Hand-Made Lace*, L. Upcott Gill, 1900

Levey, Santina M., *Lace—A History*, Victoria & Albert Museum in association with W. S. Maney & Son Ltd, 1983

Moody, A. Penderel, *Devon Pillow Lace*, Cassell & Co., 1907

Palliser, Mrs Bury, *The History of Lace*, first published Sampson, Low, Son and Marston, London, 1865 (reprinted E. P. Publishing, 1979)

Simeon, Margaret, *The History of Lace*, Stainer & Bell, 1979

Staniland, Kay and Levey, Santina M., *Queen Victoria's Wedding Dress and Lace*, in *Costume*, the journal of the Costume Society (17:1983)

Treadwin, Mrs, *Antique Point, Honiton Lace*, Ward, Lock and Tyler, 1873

Voysey, Cynthia, *Bobbin Lace in Photographs*, B. T. Batsford, 1987

Wardle, Patricia, *Victorian Lace*, Herbert Jenkins, 1968

Yallop, H. J., *The History of the Honiton Lace Industry*, University of Exeter Press, 1992

Practical

Devonia, *The Honiton Lace Book*, first published The Bazaar Office, London, c. 1870 (reprinted Paul Minet, London, 1972)

Collier, Ann, *Creative Design in Bobbin Lace*, B. T. Batsford, 1982

Earnshaw, Pat, *Bobbin and Needle Laces: Identification and Care*, B. T. Batsford, 1983

Luxton, Elsie, *The Technique of Honiton Lace*, B. T. Batsford, 1979

Luxton, Elsie, *Honiton Lace Patterns*, B.T. Batsford, 1983

Luxton, Elsie and Fukuyama, Yusai, *Honiton Lace: The Visual Approach*, B.T. Batsford, 1988

Flowers in Honiton Lace, B.T. Batsford, 1992

Maidment, Margaret, *A Manual of Hand-Made Bobbin Lace Work*, 1931, reprinted B.T. Batsford, 1983

Perryman, Pat and Voysey, Cynthia, *New Designs in Honiton Lace*, B.T. Batsford, 1984

Takano, Saikoh, *Birds and Animals in Honiton Lace*, B.T. Batsford, 1992

Thompson, Susanne, *Introduction to Honiton Lace*, B.T. Batsford, 1985

Toomer,' Heather and Voysey, Cynthia, *Lace: A Guide to Identification*, B.T. Batsford, 1989

Voysey, Cynthia, *Honiton Lace – A Practical Guide*, Bishopsgate Press Ltd, 1991

Suppliers

Books

ENGLAND

The following are stockists of the complete Batsford/Dryad Press:

AVON
Bridge Bookshop
7 Bridge Street
Bath BA2 4AS

Waterstone & Co.
4–5 Milsom Street
Bath BA1 1DA

BEDFORDSHIRE
Arthur Sells
Lane Cover
49 Pedley Lane
Clifton
Shefford SG17 5QT

BUCKINGHAMSHIRE
J. S. Sear
Lacecraft Supplies
8 Hillview
Sherington MK16 9NJ

CAMBRIDGESHIRE
Dillons the Bookstore
Sidney Street
Cambridge

CHESHIRE
Lynn Turner
Church Meadow Crafts
7 Woodford Road
Winsford

DEVON
Creative Crafts & Needlework
18 High Street
Totnes TQ9 5NP

Honiton Lace Shop
44 High Street
Honiton EX14 8PJ

DORSET
F. Herring & Sons
27 High West Street
Dorchester DT1 1UP

Tim Parker (*mail order*)
124 Corhampton Road
Boscombe East
Bournemouth BH6 5NZ

Christopher Williams
19 Morrison Avenue
Parkstone
Poole BH17 4AD

DURHAM
Lacemaid
6, 10 & 15 Stoneybeck
Bishop Middleham DL17 9BL

GLOUCESTERSHIRE
Southgate Handicrafts
63 Southgate Street
Gloucester GL1 1TX

Waterstone & Company
89–90 The Promenade
Cheltenham GL50 1NB

HAMPSHIRE
Creative Crafts
11 The Square
Winchester SO23 9ES

Doreen Gill
14 Barnfield Road
Petersfield GU31 4DR

Larkfield Crafts
4 Island Cottages
Mapledurwell
Basingstoke RG23 2LU

Needlestyle
24–26 West Street
Alresford

Ruskins
27 Bell Street
Romsey

ISLE OF WIGHT
Busy Bobbins
Unit 7
Scarrots Lane
Newport PO30 1JD

KENT
The Handicraft Shop
47 Northgate
Canterbury CT1 1BE

Hatchards
The Great Hall
Mount Pleasant Road
Tunbridge Wells

LONDON
W. & G. Foyle Ltd
113–119 Charing Cross Road
WC2H 0EB

Hatchards
187 Piccadilly W1V 9DA

MIDDLESEX
Redburn Crafts
Squires Garden Centre
Halliford Road
Upper Halliford
Shepperton TW17 8RU

NORFOLK
Alby Lace Museum
Cromer Road
Alby
Norwich NR11 7QE

Jane's Pincushions
Taverham Craft Unit 4
Taverham Nursery Centre
Fir Covert Road
Taverham
Norwich NR8 6HT

Waterstone & Company Ltd
30 London Street
Norwich NR2 1LD

NORTH YORKSHIRE
Craft Basics
9 Gillygate
York

Shireburn Lace
Finkle Court
Finkle Hill
Sherburn in Elmet LS25 6EB

The Craft House
23 Bar Street
Scarborough YO13 9QE

NORTHAMPTONSHIRE
Denis Hornsby
149 High Street
Burton Latimer
Kettering NN15 5RL

SOMERSET
Bridge Bookshop
62 Bridge Street
Taunton TA1 1UD

STAFFORDSHIRE
J. & J. Ford (*mail order & lace days only*)
October Hill
Upper Way
Upper Longdon
Rugeley WS15 1QB

SUSSEX
Waterstone & Company Ltd
120 Terminus Road
Eastbourne

WARWICKSHIRE
Christine & David Springett
21 Hillmorton Road
Rugby CV22 6DF

WEST MIDLANDS
Needlewoman
21 Needles Alley
off New Street
Birmingham B2 5AG

WEST YORKSHIRE
Sebalace
Waterloo Mill
Howden Road
Silsden BD20 0HA

George White Lacemaking Supplies
40 Heath Drive
Boston Spa LS23 6PB

Just Lace
Lacemaker Supplies
14 Ashwood Gardens
Gildersome
Leeds LS27 7AS

Jo Firth
58 Kent Crescent
Lowtown, Pudsey
Leeds LS28 9EB

WILTSHIRE
Everyman Bookshop
5 Bridge Street
Salisbury SP1 2ND

SCOTLAND
Embroidery Shop
51 William Street
Edinburgh
Lothian EH3 7LW

Waterstone & Company Ltd
236 Union Street
Aberdeen AB1 1TN

WALES
Bryncraft Bobbins (*mail order*)
B. J. Phillips
Pantglas
Cellan
Lampeter
Dyfed SA48 8JD

Hilkar Lace Suppliers
33 Mysydd Road
Landore
Swansea

Equipment

UNITED KINGDOM

BEDFORDSHIRE
A. Sells
49 Pedley Lane
Clifton
Shefford SG17 5QT

BERKSHIRE
Chrisken Bobbins
26 Cedar Drive
Kingsclere RG15 8TD

BUCKINGHAMSHIRE
J. S. Sear
Lacecraft Supplies
8 Hillview
Sherington MK16 9NJ

SMP
4 Garners Close
Chalfont St Peter SL9 0HB

Winslow Bobbins
70 Magpie Way
Winslow MK18 3PZ

CAMBRIDGESHIRE
Josie and Jeff Harrison
Walnut Cottage
Winwick
Huntingdon PE17 5PP

Spangles
Carole Morris
Cashburn Lane
Burwell CB5 0ED

CHESHIRE
Lynn Turner
Church Meadow Crafts
7 Woodford Road
Winsford

DEVON
Honiton Lace Shop
44 High Street
Honiton EX14 8PJ

DORSET
Frank Herring & Sons
27 High West Street
Dorchester DT1 1UP

Tim Parker (*mail order, general and bobbins*)
124 Corhampton Road
Boscombe East
Bournemouth BH6 5NZ

ESSEX
Needlework
Ann Bartleet
Bucklers Farm
Coggeshall CO6 1SB

GLOUCESTERSHIRE
Chosen Crafts Centre
46 Winchcombe Street
Cheltenham GL52 2ND

HAMPSHIRE
Busy Bobbins
Unit 7
Scarrots Lane
Newport
IOW PO30 1JD

Needlestyle
24–26 West Street
Alresford

Newnham Lace Equipment (*lace pillows*)
15 Marlowe Close
Basingstoke RG24 9DD

KENT
The Handicraft Shop
47 Northgate
Canterbury CT1 1BE

Denis Hornsby
25 Manwood Avenue
Canterbury CT2 7AH

Frances Iles
73 High Street
Rochester ME1 1LX

LINCOLNSHIRE
Ken and Pat Schultz
Whynacres
Shepeau Stow
Whaplode Drove
Spalding PE12 0TU

MERSEYSIDE
Hayes & Finch
Head Office & Factory
Hanson Road
Aintree
Liverpool L9 9BP

MIDDLESEX
Redburn Crafts
Squires Garden Centre
Halliford Road
Upper Halliford
Shepperton TW17 8RU

NORFOLK
Alby Lace Museum
Cromer Road
Alby
Norwich NR11 7QE

Jane's Pincushions
Taverham Craft Unit 4
Taverham Nursery Centre
Fir Covert Road
Taverham
Norwich NR8 6HT

George Walker
The Corner Shop
Rickinghall, Diss

NORTH HUMBERSIDE
Teazle Embroideries
35 Boothferry Road
Hull

NORTH YORKSHIRE
The Craft House
23 Bar Street
Scarborough

Shireburn Lace
Finkle Court
Finkle Hill
Sherburn in Elmet LS25 6EB

Stitchery
Finkle Street
Richmond

SOUTH YORKSHIRE
D. H. Shaw
47 Lamor Crescent
Thrushcroft
Rotherham S66 9QD

STAFFORDSHIRE
J. & J. Ford (*mail order and lace days only*)
October Hill
Upper Way
Upper Longdon
Rugeley WS15 1QB

SUFFOLK
E. & J. Piper (*silk embroidery and lace thread*)
Silverlea
Flax Lane
Glemsford CO10 7RS

SURREY
Needle and Thread
80 High Street
Horsell
Woking GU21 4SZ

Needlestyle
5 The Woolmead
Farnham GU9 7TX

SUSSEX
Southern Handicrafts
20 Kensington Gardens
Brighton BN1 4AC

WARWICKSHIRE
Christine & David Springett
21 Hillmorton Road
Rugby CV22 5DF

WEST MIDLANDS
Framecraft
83 Hampstead Road
Handsworth Wood
Birmingham B2 1JA

The Needlewoman
21 Needles Alley
off New Street
Birmingham B2 5AE

Stitches
Dovehouse Shopping Parade
Warwick Road
Olton, Solihull

WEST YORKSHIRE
Jo Firth
Lace Marketing & Needlecraft Supplies
58 Kent Crescent
Lowtown
Pudsey LS28 9EB

Just Lace
Lacemaker Supplies
14 Ashwood Gardens
Gildersome
Leeds LS27 7AS

Sebalace
Waterloo Mills
Howden Road
Silsden BD20 0HA

George White Lacemaking Supplies
40 Heath Drive
Boston Spa LS23 6PB

SCOTLAND
Christine Riley
53 Barclay Street
Stonehaven
Kincardineshire

Peter & Beverley Scarlett
Strupak
Hill Head
Cold Well, Ellon
Grampian

WALES
Bryncraft Bobbins
B. J. Phillips
Pantglas
Cellan
Lampeter
Dyfed SA48 8JD

Hilkar Lace Suppliers
33 Mysydd Road
Landore
Swansea

AUSTRALIA
Australian Lace magazine
P.O. Box 1291
Toowong
Queensland 4066

Dentelles Lace Supplies
c/o Betty Franks
39 Lang Terrace
Northgate 4013
Brisbane
Queensland

The Lacemaker
724a Riversdale Road
Camberwell
Victoria 3124

Spindle and Loom
83 Longueville Road
Lane Cove
NSW 2066

Tulis Crafts
201 Avoca Street
Randwick
NSW 2031

NEW ZEALAND
Peter McLeavey
P.O. Box 69.007
Auckland 8

USA
Arbor House
22 Arbor Lane
Roslyn Heights
NY 11577

Baltazor Inc.
3262 Severn Avenue
Metairie
LA 7002

Beggars' Lace
P.O. Box 481223
Denver
Colo 80248

Berga Ullman Inc.
P.O. Box 918
North Adams
MA 01247

Happy Hands
3007 S. W. Marshall
Pendleton
Oreg 97180

International Old Lacers
P.O. Box 1029
Westminster
CO 80030

The Lacemaker
23732–G Bothell Hwy, SE
Bothell
WA 98021

Lace Place de Belgique
800 S. W. 17th Street
Boca Raton
FL 33432

Lacis
3163 Adeline Street
Berkeley
CA 94703

Robin's Bobbins
RT1 Box 1736
Mineral Bluff
GA 30559–9736

Robin and Russ
Handweavers
533 North Adams Street
McMinnville
Oreg 97128

Van Sciver Bobbin Lace
130 Cascadilla Park
Ithaca
NY 14850

The World in Stitches
82 South Street
Milford
N.H. 03055

Sources of Information

UNITED KINGDOM

The British College of Lace
21 Hillmorton Road
Rugby
War CV22 5DF

The Lace Guild
The Hollies
53 Audnam
Stourbridge
West Midlands DY8 4AE

The Lacemakers' Circle
49 Wardwick
Derby DE1 1HY

The Lace Society
Linwood
Stratford Road
Oversley
Alcester
War BY9 6PG

Ring of Tatters
Miss B. Netherwood
269 Oregon Way
Chaddesden
Derby DE2 6UR

United Kingdom Director of International Old Lacers
S. Hurst
4 Dollis Road
London N3 1RG

USA

International Old Lacers
Gunvor Jorgensen (Pres.)
366 Bradley Avenue
Northvale
NR 076647

Lace & Crafts magazine
3201 East Lakeshore Drive
Tallahassee
FL 32312–2034

OIDFA
(International Bobbin and Needle Lace Organization)
Kathy Kauffmann
1301 Greenwood
Wilmette
Illinois 60091

Index